COOKING SLOW

COOKING
· SLOW ·

RECIPES *for* SLOWING DOWN *and* COOKING MORE

Andrew Schloss

Photographs by **Alan Benson**

CHRONICLE BOOKS
SAN FRANCISCO

Library of Congress Cataloging-in-Publication Data available.

ISBN 978-1-4521-0469-0

Manufactured in China

Designed by Laura Palese and Alice Chau
Typesetting by Howie Severson

10 9 8 7 6 5 4 3 2 1

Chronicle Books LLC
680 Second Street
San Francisco, California 94107
www.chroniclebooks.com

To Xander

INTRODUCTION

AN INVITATION TO RELAX

Cooking is a balance between time and temperature. Raise the heat and everything speeds up: flames jump, pots sizzle, grease spits. Lower the heat, however, and the turmoil subsides. Time stretches. Tough fibers soften. Beautifully complex flavors emerge. Aromas billow, and all you have to do is slow down and relax. That's the magic of slow cooking.

Reconsidering this balance in the kitchen suggests a simple formula that can play out in many areas of our lives. The daily task of making dinner starts to shift. Your house transforms with heart-warming aromas, your family experiences genuinely delicious home-cooked meals, and you learn that by allowing food to cook untended all day, your work is reduced to minutes, while the good ingredients you purchased are being transformed in ways that only time can accomplish.

In a world where convenience is synonymous with speed, slowing down to save time seems like an oxymoron . . . but that is exactly what happens when you start to incorporate slow-cooking recipes into your cooking repertoire. You can set up a chicken for gentle roasting or a slow-baked casserole after morning coffee and bring it to the table at suppertime with little thought and no effort in between. You can be occupied elsewhere while your dinner simmers lazily, and by turning your oven or stove top into a slow cooker you find out that you can spend all day cooking, hands-free, with no sacrifice of quality, and no fear of overcooking.

LOW-TEMPERATURE COOKING

The term "slow cooking" captures the style and the principle of the process, but behind its magical results is simply the science of low-temperature cooking. Let's use roast beef as a prime example. The doneness temperature of a medium-rare rib roast is 130°F/55°C, meaning the protein in the meat has just begun to firm, making the meat resilient to the touch; the texture of the meat has lost its raw slickness but it is still moist and the juices flow from the meat when it is cut. The interior color has turned from dark to lighter red. If the beef was roasted in a 350°F/180°C/gas 4 oven, the exterior of the roast would have reached temperatures way above medium-rare in order for the center to get to the perfect temperature. At 400°F/200°C/gas 6, the changes to the outside of the roast would be even greater, and at that temperature misjudging timing could result in rapid overcooking.

But if the oven temperature is set at 130°F/55°C, the roast can never get any hotter than medium-rare. It is impossible to overcook it, even if it were left roasting for days. By moving the cooking temperature close to the doneness temperature, we minimize the danger of overcooking, which allows us to extend the cooking time to better fit a flexible schedule.

The advantage is much more than a matter of convenient timing. By keeping the temperature moderate, proteins firm more gently, making finished meats more tender, custards softer, fish moister, and casseroles creamier. The textural improvements from low-temperature cooking are remarkable, and yet many dishes cooked in a slow cooker come out mushy rather than succulent. The culprit is the water.

SLOW COOKERS VS. SLOW COOKING

The biggest difference between slow cooking in a slow cooker and any other piece of cooking equipment is water. There is much less evaporation from a slow cooker than there is from a saucepan or a skillet simmering on a stove top. The heat of a slow cooker is separated from the cooking vessel by a cushion of air, so the heat in a slow cooker is much more diffuse than the heat on a stove top; the liquid inside therefore transforms into steam more gradually. In addition, slow-cooker lids are usually made of glass, designed to stay relatively cool

so that the steam rising from the cooking food precipitates back into water on the inside of the cooler lid, instead of sizzling away, as it would on the metal top of a Dutch oven, and drips back into the food.

This closed moisture system ensures that the heat in the cooker remains constant and the ingredients stay moist, one of the great advantages of cooking in a slow cooker. But it is not faultless and can be challenging to get perfect results, as preserving moisture inhibits flavors from concentrating. One of the principal ways that flavor develops in traditional cooking is through water evaporation: As the percentage of water reduces in a sauce, stew, or soup, the concentration of flavorful elements increases. At the same time, the percentage of solid particles increases and the liquid thickens. When slow-cooking in a slow cooker, neither happens, so the only way to end up with intense, dynamic flavors and smooth, creamy textures is to make sure they're there before the slow cooker ever gets turned on. This is why slow-cooker recipes usually contain very little liquid and a generous amount of seasoning.

All of these drawbacks are eliminated by switching to slow cooking on a stove top or in an oven. Because ovens have lots of hot air between the food and the heating element, there is ample space for evaporation, so ingredients that are slow-roasted or slow-baked in an oven develop better flavor and richer textures than in a slow cooker.

The difference between roasting and baking (whether slow or fast) is largely semantic these days. At one time, roasting meant hanging a haunch of meat on a spit over an open fire. By keeping the meat at a distance from the flame, you could control the temperature and avoid burning it before it cooked through. By contrast, baking was done in metal or ceramic vessels placed to one side of the fire or buried in the smoldering coals. Food was placed in the pot, where it was protected from flame and could cook through without fear of scorching.

In time, ovens became large, freestanding units that could fit whole roasts, and eventually they took preference over the fireplace for roasting meat, largely because ovens did not require constant tending. Since then, the terms "roasting" and "baking" have become confused. For my purposes (aside from doughs, batters, and casseroles, all of which I "bake"), I "roast" whole meats and "bake" smaller cuts. For instance I would call the method for cooking a whole chicken "roasting" but refer to the method of cooking chicken parts as "baking." But these distinctions are barely consistent. Like many other people, I "roast" vegetables even though they are almost always cut up, probably because they are cooked at a high enough temperature to scorch the edges, a traditional mark of roasting rather than baking.

The other common technique for slow cooking is simmering or braising, which can be done either on a stove top or in an oven. Both cook food in liquid, which helps to keep it moist, but more important, the presence of liquid controls temperature and timing. The maximum temperature of boiling water is 212°F/100°C, no matter how much heat is applied to the pan; that is, as long as there is water present, submerged food can't get hotter than 212°F/100°C. The technique just requires vigilance at the boiling point, when water is rapidly evaporating into steam and must be replenished regularly. In slow braising and simmering, the temperatures are kept far below a boil, so, for example, a brisket or pork shoulder simmering at 160 to 180°F/71 to 82°C

can cook all day without losing moisture and without overcooking—the temperature of the liquid never gets hotter than you want the meat to be when it is done. Braising or simmering tougher cuts of muscled meats at these lower temperatures produces far more tender results than traditional braising temperatures.

Steaming and frying are less common slow-cooking techniques, mostly because their timing can't be stretched indefinitely, and therefore you have to be more attentive to keep ingredients from overcooking. However, by slowing them down, you get the same textural benefits that happen with other slow-cooking techniques.

HOW TO USE THIS BOOK

The chapters are divided by slow cooking method: roasting, baking, simmering, steaming, grilling, and frying, followed by two chapters on cooking in slow-cooking appliances (slow cookers and sous vide), and a chapter on desserts. Specific tips and advice for each type of slow-cooking method are covered in recipes and in each chapter introduction. I recognize that most people think slow cooking can only be done in a slow cooker, and though this book emphasizes foods that can be cooked in a slow cooker, the recipes either improve or match the results achieved in a slow cooker by cooking in a low oven or gently on a stove top. These include slow-cooking recipes for roasts, egg dishes, and sweets that would be ruined by a slow cooker. When appropriate, I have included separate instructions for cooking many of the recipes in a slow cooker.

Two chapters here are devoted to recipes that are cooked in one of two slow-cooking appliances: a slow cooker or a sous vide cooker. There are countless slow-cooker books (including mine, *Art of the Slow Cooker*), so it is easy to find recipes for these machines. For that reason, and because my passionate exploration here is for the beauties of other slow-cooking techniques, I have included only recipes that I believe are better cooked in a slow cooker than by any other method. Professional sous vide machines have been around for several decades, but only recently have been manufactured for the home kitchen, which is also an exciting development for adventurous home cooks. Sous vide machines are similar to slow cookers, except they can be set to far lower temperatures. In the next section, I will explain slow cookers and sous vide cookers in greater detail.

Timing is given for each recipe broken down between prep time (assembling ingredients, chopping, etc.) and cooking time (some sautéing but most of the time you can walk away). If the ingredients need chilling or resting, that is listed separately, as are guidelines for storage and reheating. If you need additional special equipment, that is listed separately.

Cooking times are intentionally stated with lots of leeway. In most of these recipes the cooking temperatures are so low and the method so forgiving that an extra hour or two will not make a marked difference.

SMALL EQUIPMENT

Slow cookers are designed to cook at a constant low temperature, but you don't have to use a slow cooker to get all of the advantages of this popular style of cooking. A covered pot in an oven set at 200°F/95°C provides the same cooking environment as a slow cooker set on low. The same can be said for a covered casserole placed in a pot of simmering water, or a gently warmed pot of olive oil set over a low flame. Without losing the ease of a slow cooker, slow baking, roasting, steaming, simmering, and frying can expand your slow-cooking opportunities into every part of the kitchen. Each method has its advantages and limitations.

Cast-Iron Skillet

A large cast-iron skillet with a tight-fitting lid is an alternative to a Dutch oven. Except for its flatter, wider shape, the two pots perform identically and require the same care to prevent rusting.

Dutch Oven

The Dutch oven is the most versatile piece of slow-cooking equipment you can own. It can be used on a stove top, in an oven, on a grill, or in an open fire, for sautéing, braising, stewing, baking, roasting, frying, and steaming. A Dutch oven is an all-purpose cooking pot (usually made of iron) with a tight-fitting lid and protrusions on either side of the rim that can either be used as handles or as anchors for a hanging (bail) handle. Originally designed for cooking in an open fire, early Dutch ovens often had feet to lift the bottom of the pot over the hot coals on the floor of a fireplace. Early Dutch oven lids are either flat or concave so that coals can be piled on top. This allowed the pot to act like a small oven for baking, with heat coming from all sides.

If your Dutch oven is raw cast iron, it should be seasoned with oil for its initial use (most come preseasoned). Before seasoning, the iron will be gray and dull, and afterward it will become black and shiny. After each use, the pot should be gently washed, not scrubbed, dried thoroughly (setting the pot on a low burner until dry is the easiest way), and rubbed with a thin film of vegetable oil to maintain the seasoned surface and to keep the iron from rusting. Some Dutch ovens are coated in brightly colored enamel. These are not as good at browning (enamel is a poor heat conductor), but they do not require seasoning or oiling. And they will not rust.

Slow Cookers

Slow cookers consist of three parts: a metal casing that contains an electric heating element and heat controls, a ceramic insert that fits inside the metal casing, and a lid. The ceramic material heats up slowly and gives off heat gradually. Provided that the heat source is steady and controlled, a ceramic pot can warm food to a set temperature and keep it there for hours without fear of scorching or overheating.

On the other hand, ceramics are terrible at browning or searing. In cooking, brown is not just a color; it is a flavor, the flavor of succulence, which is why most good slow-cooker recipes start by browning ingredients in a metal pan. During browning, sugars and proteins on the surface of meats and vegetables caramelize, transforming into hundreds of highly charged aromatic flavor components.

There are some "brown and cook" slow cookers containing inserts with sufficient heat-transferring properties to be used on a stove top (with a heat diffuser) so that you can brown ingredients in the same pot in which they will be slow-cooked. Though this seems like a breakthrough, the technology has its limitations. For one thing, the insert doesn't brown nearly as well as a metal pan and it has a tendency to transfer heat too quickly during slow cooking, exacerbating the danger of scorching over a 6- to 8-hour cooking span. A cast-iron skillet or Dutch oven that can be used for browning ingredients on a stove top and then put in a low oven for slow cooking does a better job than "brown and cook" slow-cooker crockery.

Although all slow cookers operate similarly, there are differences, more between models than between brands. When choosing a slow cooker, you will need to consider:

SIZE: Slow cookers range in size from 1 to 8 qt/1.5 to 7.5 l, although most are between 3 and 6 qt/3.5 and 5.7 l. You should always use a slow cooker that fits the amount of food you are cooking. For best results, the crockery should be filled to at least one-third of its volume and no more than three-fourths full.

CONTROLS: Basic slow cookers have three settings: low (heats between 185 and 200°F/85 and 93°C), high (heats between 250 and 300°F/121 and 149°C), and off. Many models also have a warm setting that holds the contents at about 165°F/74°C. None of these cookers keeps track of time; once you set them up and turn them on, they stay at one setting until they are manually switched. Several years ago, programmable slow cookers were introduced that automatically switch to warm at a set time. The early versions have four time settings: 4 or 6 hours on high, and 8 or 10 hours on low. Now there are several brands of programmable slow cookers that

allow you to set timing by half hour or minute increments (from 1 minute to 20 hours). At the set time they will switch to warm, but they cannot switch from high to low or switch off automatically. These machines tend to cost three to four times more than nonprogrammable models.

HEATING: Although all slow cookers say that their low setting is about 200°F/95°C and high is 300°F/149°C, the truth is that there is a wide range. To test how well your slow cooker heats, put 2 qt/2 l of room-temperature water in the cooker, cover, and turn to low. After 3 hours the water should be hotter than 140°F/60°C, and after 6 hours it should be at least 180°F/82°C. Older slow cookers will tend to top out on low at around 185°F/85°C; newer ones will get to slightly hotter than 200°F/93°C. If your cooker is hotter or lower than these mark points, adjust your cooking times accordingly. If they are much lower, buy a new cooker; the one you have is not heating fast enough to ensure that the food you are cooking is safe.

BRANDS: There are more than a dozen major manufacturers of slow cookers, and most of them have several models, making the choices seem endless. In my experience, no brand is categorically better than another, and since they are all introducing several new models every year it is impossible to predict what the future holds. The best advice is to ask your friends, look at consumer feedback, consider your needs, and seek sales; you probably won't go wrong.

Soufflé Dish or Pudding Mold

Used for baking puddings and cakes, these straight-sided molds can be made of ceramic or metal. Pudding molds are often embossed or shaped decoratively and have tight-fitting lids.

Sous Vide Cookers

Sous vide appliances cook similarly to slow cookers, except, rather dramatically, the food is submerged in heated water. The machines can be set to cook at very low temperatures, as low as 130°F/54°C. This allows you to slow-cook rare meats, soft-cooked eggs, and delicate fish that would be ruined if cooked at the low setting of a slow cooker.

Because the food is submerged in water, it must be sealed to protect it. The term *sous vide* means "under pressure," referring to the process of vacuum sealing ingredients in plastic before they are cooked. The vacuum seal keeps air and microorganisms away from the food and ensures that the pouches stay submerged during cooking. Because the pouch is surrounded by water that is heated to the exact temperature you want the food to be when it is done, overcooking is eliminated and all of the advantages of slow cooking that I have been extolling throughout these pages take place automatically.

There are several home devices for vacuum sealing. The most popular is made by FoodSaver, and comes with food-grade plastic pouches (pouches are also available separately at most big box stores, kitchen supply stores, or online). A vacuum sealer can also be used to vacuum wrap fresh food, which will greatly increase its storage life.

There are two types of sous vide cooking appliances. The less expensive option is known commonly by its brand name, SousVide Supreme. This type of sous vide device is a cubic double-walled vessel, with a tight-fitting insulating lid, and a control panel on the front, making it look like a squared-off rice cooker. To use it, you fill the vessel with water and set the temperature on the control panel. When the water bath reaches the set temperature, you add the sealed food, close the lid, and walk away. The more expensive, and more professional, sous vide option is called a thermal circulator, and is sold as Sous Vide by PolyScience. As the name implies, the circulator contains a pump that circulates the water in the cooker, ensuring that the temperature is even throughout. The still water bath of a SousVide Supreme can have hot and cold spots that differ from the set temperature. The thermal circulator does not come with its own vessel, but can clip on to any large pot, making it lightweight and easy to store.

Because the cooking temperatures in sous vide can be very low, food safety is more of a concern than it is in other forms of slow cooking. When meat is roasted at 300°F/150°C/ gas 2, any bacteria on the surface of the meat is quickly killed, but in sous vide that doesn't happen, so meats are often seared to kill any bacteria, and then chilled to under 40°F/4°C before being sealed.

Steaming Basket

These perforated containers are either perched on the rim of a pot of steaming liquid or are equipped with legs so that they can be inserted into the pot and hold the food above the steaming liquid. Steaming baskets can be made of stainless steel or bamboo. Metal steamers last longer but bamboo steamers absorb precipitating steam and thereby keep water droplets from collecting on the surface of the food.

LARGE EQUIPMENT

Grills

You can slow-cook on a charcoal or gas grill (see page 130), but you will need a grill with a cover and a grilling area large enough to split in two, part for the fire and an area away from the fire for cooking the food. This setup, known as indirect grilling, turns your grill into a sort of oven. For indirect grilling, you will need a medium-size kettle grill, a gas grill with two or more burners, or a barrel grill that has an offset fire box separate from the grilling area. Hibachi and small tabletop grills are usually too small for indirect grilling.

Ovens

The oven is the most versatile tool for slow cooking. It requires minimal energy and because the heating element is enclosed within the oven's walls there is no danger of an open flame. The oven can be used for many forms of slow cooking, including baking, roasting, simmering, steaming, and frying.

The lowest possible setting for most ovens is 175°F/80°C. The doneness temperature of many meats is lower than this, so it is not possible to slow-roast beef, lamb, or pork at its doneness temperature. Still, roasting at 175°F/80°C will give you far more moisture retention and tenderizing effects than roasting at higher temperatures.

Because food can slow-cook for hours in an oven, it is important that your oven's thermostat is accurate. Calibrate the oven by testing its internal temperature with an oven thermometer placed in the middle of the oven. Set the thermostat to 200°F/95°C, and when the oven is up to temperature, check the thermometer. If it is off by more than 2 degrees, you can adjust the thermostat accordingly or have the oven professionally calibrated. Electric ovens usually heat more evenly and have less dramatic temperature cycles than gas ovens.

Stove Tops

Successful slow cooking over an open burner requires some trial and error. Because there is no way to determine the exact temperature of stove top burners, you will have to experiment to determine the best settings for maintaining a gentle simmer or slow steam with your equipment. The stove top recipes in this book include visual cues to look for in the food that will help you determine if your heat is at the proper level. If you are cooking with gas, you will need to use the full range of your burner, down to the smallest flame. If you have an electric stove top, a heat diffuser can be of considerable help at regulating very low heat.

FOOD SAFETY

Bacteria grow most rapidly between 40°F/4°C (refrigerator temperature) and 140°F/60°C (the temperature of very hot tap water). Most bacteria in food are beneficial, and there are many instances, making yogurt or fermenting pickles for example, when we encourage the growth of bacteria.

But the danger of harmful bacterial contamination is severe enough that minimizing the presence of bacteria and moving edibles out of the temperature danger zone quickly are major concerns. The most at-risk foods in this arena are proteins, so when slow-cooking whole pieces of meat, fish, and poultry, it is common practice to either salt the outside of the meat and refrigerate it for enough time to neutralize bacteria, or to brown the ingredient before slow-cooking it to kill surface bacteria. Treating the surfaces of whole pieces of wholesome meat is sufficient, because harmful bacteria only have access to the outside of these meats.

Ground meat and liquid proteins are a different story. Ground meats should not be slow-cooked unless they have been heavily salted (as is done in sausage making), or thoroughly browned. Liquid proteins, like milk or cream, should be pasteurized if they are going to be used in slow cooking.

Once the danger of preexisting bacteria has been mitigated, slow roasting can proceed without further concern, but when slow-cooking liquids, like soup, stew, or something baked in a sauce, contamination can continue to occur during the early phases of cooking, before the food has reached the 140°F/60°C safety benchmark. Cooking these recipes at high temperatures for the first 10 to 15 minutes goes a long way toward maintaining safety, and keeping the preparation above 140°F/60°C for an hour or more ensures any bacteria that could still be present is killed.

CHAPTER 1

SLOW
ROASTING

Jean Anthelme Brillat-Savarin, the famous French gastronome, in his landmark treatise *La Physiologie du Goût* (*The Physiology of Taste*), written in 1825, said "A man may be taught how to cook, but he must be born knowing how to roast." Get ready to be reborn.

Roasting involves little more than putting food in a preheated oven and giving it its privacy until it is done. Roasting meat at medium or high temperatures, between 350 and 450°F/175 and 230°C, browns the surface quickly and deeply, which makes the roast look and taste delicious, but it also causes a lot of moisture loss. The exterior gets far hotter than the interior, and the center can move from medium-rare to medium-well in a matter of minutes. Even after a roast is removed from the oven, the hotter surface areas continue to transfer heat into the center, which is why meat that has been roasted at a high temperature has to be removed from the oven when it is about 10°F/5°C below its ideal doneness temperature (see chart, opposite) and should rest for 10 to 20 minutes (depending on the size of the roast) to reach its ideal temperature.

Lowering the oven thermostat below 200°F/95°C does just the opposite. The formation of a crust is diminished, but so is moisture loss, resulting in a juicier, more evenly done interior, less shrinkage, and a long leeway time before the meat overcooks. To make up for the lack of browning, slow-roasted meats can be browned before or after roasting, either in a hot oven for 10 minutes or by being sautéed briefly on a stove top.

Lowering the heat also gives the meat's own protein-tenderizing enzymes more time to work, making slow roasting the preferred method for tenderizing tougher, larger roasts, like bottom round or chuck roasts. The combination of time, moisture, and active enzymes in slow roasting gradually turns the tough connective tissue in meat, called collagen, into gelatin. Gelatin has a luscious, rich mouthfeel, which is what gives sauces and gravies made from pan drippings their silky texture. Slow roasting retains that richness in the meat itself.

MEAT DONENESS

MEAT	BLUE	RARE	MEDIUM-RARE	MEDIUM	MEDIUM-WELL	WELL-DONE
BEEF STEAK	120°F/ 49°C	125°F/ 52°C	135°F/ 57°C	145°F/ 63°C	155°F/ 68°C	170°F/ 77°C
BEEF ROAST	115°F/ 46°C	125°F/ 52°C	135°F/ 57°C	145°F/ 63°C	155°F/ 68°C	170°F/ 77°C
BEEF TOUGH CUTS					155°F/ 68°C	170°F/ 77°C
GROUND BEEF					150°F/ 66°C	160°F/ 71°C
PORK CHOPS					155°F/ 68°C	170°F/ 77°C
PORK ROAST					155°F/ 68°C	170°F/ 77°C
PORK SHOULDER					165°F/ 74°C	170°F/ 77°C
GROUND PORK					155°F/ 68°C	165°F/ 74°C
LAMB CHOPS	120°F/ 49°C	125°F/ 52°C	135°F/ 57°C	145°F/ 63°C	155°F/ 68°C	170°F/ 77°C
LAMB ROASTS	115°F/ 46°C	125°F/ 52°C	135°F/ 57°C	145°F/ 63°C	155°F/ 68°C	170°F/ 77°C
LAMB SHOULDER					155°F/ 68°C	170°F/ 77°C
GROUND LAMB					150°F/ 66°C	160°F/ 71°C
VEAL CHOPS			135°F/ 57°C	145°F/ 63°C	155°F/ 68°C	170°F/ 77°C
VEAL ROASTS			135°F/ 57°C	145°F/ 63°C	155°F/ 68°C	170°F/ 77°C
VEAL SHANKS					155°F/ 68°C	170°F/ 77°C
GROUND VEAL					150°F/ 66°C	160°F/ 71°C
POULTRY					170°F/ 77°C	180°F/ 82°C
FISH				140°F/ 60°C	150°F/ 66°C	160°F/ 71°C

SLOW-ROASTED
CHICKEN
WITH SUN-DRIED TOMATOES AND WILD MUSHROOMS

Dried vegetables are convenient (they keep in a pantry for months); they are also flavor bombs (getting rid of the water concentrates their flavorful components). The only downside is that these shriveled beauties need to hydrate before they can be eaten, which usually requires a preliminary soaking step. But not in slow roasting. All roasting extracts juices from a bird, but slow roasting does it so gradually that the liquid doesn't evaporate immediately. Instead it drips into the pan, where, in this recipe, it is sucked into a bed of dried mushrooms and tomatoes, plumping the vegetables with its savory juices.

PREP TIME: 15 minutes	COOKING TIME: 6¼ to 8¼ hours	STORE: for up to 3 days, covered in the refrigerator. Reheat gently in a low oven.	*Makes* 4 TO 6 *servings*

» 1 chicken, about 4 lb/1.8 kg, preferably free-range

» Coarse sea salt and freshly ground black pepper

» 4 fresh rosemary sprigs

» 2 tbsp olive oil

» 1 large yellow onion, peeled and cut into 8 to 10 chunks

» 6 garlic cloves, halved

» ½ cup/120 ml full-bodied red wine such as Cabernet Sauvignon or Merlot

» 1 cup/25 g mixed dried wild mushrooms such as porcini, morels, oysters, and/or shiitake

» ½ cup/55 g chopped sun-dried tomatoes

» ¼ cup/60 ml boiling water

» 3 tbsp light brown sugar

» 1½ tbsp balsamic vinegar

» 2 tbsp chopped fresh flat-leaf parsley

Preheat the oven to 175°F/80°C.

Remove the giblets from the chicken and discard (or save for another use). Rinse the chicken inside and out and pat dry with paper towels. Season inside and out with salt and pepper and insert 2 of the rosemary sprigs inside the body cavity; set aside.

In a Dutch oven or other large, ovenproof pot with a lid, heat the olive oil over medium heat. Add the onion and sauté until tender and turning golden in spots, about 5 minutes. Add the garlic and sauté until aromatic, about 3 minutes. Add the wine, bring to a boil, and simmer until the alcohol aroma dissipates, about 2 minutes. Add the mushrooms, tomatoes, and boiling water and stir to mix well. Tear the leaves from the remaining 2 rosemary sprigs and scatter over the top.

Nestle the chicken atop the bed of vegetables and cover the pot. Transfer to the oven and roast until an instant-read thermometer inserted into the thickest part of a thigh (but not touching bone) registers 170°F/77°C, 6 to 8 hours.

Raise the oven temperature to 500°F/260°C/gas 10. In a small bowl, whisk together the brown sugar and vinegar. Remove the chicken from the oven, uncover, and brush all over with the brown sugar mixture. Return to the oven, uncovered, and roast until the chicken is nicely browned, 10 to 15 minutes longer.

Using two large, sturdy spatulas, lift the chicken out of the pot and transfer to a carving board. Carve into serving pieces. Add the parsley to the vegetables and pan drippings and stir to blend. Divide the chicken pieces among dinner plates, scoop the vegetables on the side, and serve.

SLOW-ROASTED
CHICKEN
WITH POTATOES AND HERBS

Chicken roasted with potatoes—nothing is more delicious, or easier. Pulling off this classic pair as a slow roast is bit more complicated, but completely foolproof nonetheless. It is literally impossible to overcook the bird, which is exactly the way most roast chickens go astray. The wrinkle lies with the potatoes: they will never get done at the low temperature that's ideal for roasting chicken, so they need to be precooked. This creates an extra step, but it is a simple one, and entirely worth the absence of hovering and fuss during the leisurely march to tenderness and flavor.

SEASONING TIME: 1 to 12 hours **PREP TIME:** 10 min	**COOK TIME:** 4 to 6 hours, 40 minutes	**STORE:** for up to 3 days, covered in the refrigerator. Reheat gently in a low oven.	*Makes* **4** *servings*

» 1 chicken, about 4 lb/1.8 kg, preferably organic free-range

» Coarse sea salt

» Freshly ground black pepper

» ¼ cup/10 g chopped fresh herbs such as flat-leaf parsley, rosemary, or thyme, or a combination

» 2 garlic cloves, minced

» 2 tbsp olive oil

» 2 lb/910 g russet potatoes, scrubbed but not peeled, cut into slices ½ in/12 mm thick

» 1 medium yellow onion, halved lengthwise and cut into slices ¼ in/6 mm thick

Remove the giblets from the chicken and discard (or save for another use). Rinse the chicken inside and out and pat dry with paper towels.

At least 1 hour before you plan to start roasting the chicken or up to the night before, season the chicken inside and out with 2 tsp salt and 1 tsp pepper. If starting more than 1 hour ahead, refrigerate the chicken, uncovered, up to 12 hours; remove from the refrigerator 1 hour before you plan to start roasting, to take the chill off.

Preheat the oven to 450°F/230°C/gas 8. In a small bowl, stir together the herbs and garlic; set aside.

Heat the olive oil in a large cast-iron skillet over high heat until very hot. Working in batches to cook in a single layer without the slices overlapping, cook the potatoes until nicely browned on both sides in batches so that the slices do not overlap. When browned, remove to a plate and brown the rest.

Lower the heat to medium, add the onion and sauté until tender and lightly browned. Return the potatoes to the pan, season with salt and pepper and one-third of the herb mixture, and toss to coat.

CONTINUED

Rub the remaining herb mixture all over the chicken. Place breast-side down on the potatoes and roast in the preheated oven for 15 minutes. Reduce the oven temperature to 175°F/80°C, turn the chicken breast-side up, return to the oven, and roast until a thermometer inserted into a thigh registers 170°F/77°C, 4 to 6 hours. Timing is not crucial; at that temperature the chicken will not overcook.

To finish, raise the oven temperature to 500°F/260°C/gas 10 and roast until the skin of the chicken is brown and crisp, about 10 minutes.

Carve the chicken into serving pieces and serve with the potatoes.

BALSAMIC-GLAZED

DUCKLING

Duck has a fat problem; there's a lot of it on these buoyant birds, and much of it lies in hidden places. By all rights, then, the bird should sizzle during roasting, the skin turning into a crispy layer that yields decadently to succulent meat beneath. But too often, just the opposite happens: the skin stays flabby while the meat overcooks. Here again, slowing down is the perfect solution. By reducing the oven to 175°F/80°C, the doneness temperature of roasted duck, you give the thick layer of fat ample time to melt while ducking, if you will, the high temperatures that lead to overcooking.

Salting the duck a day ahead helps to soften the fat and dry out the skin, and starting roasting at a high temperature accelerates both desirable factors.

CHILLING TIME: 12 to 24 hours PREP TIME: 5 minutes	COOKING TIME: 4½ to 6½ hours	STORE: for up to 3 days, covered in the refrigerator. Reheat gently in a low oven.	*Makes* **6** *servings*

» **2 ducks such as Muscovy or Pekin, about 4 lb/1.8 kg each**

» **4 tsp coarse sea salt**

» **2 tsp freshly ground black pepper**

» **8 garlic cloves, minced**

» **½ cup/120 ml balsamic vinegar**

Remove the giblets from the ducks and discard (or save for another use). Rinse the ducks inside and out and pat dry with paper towels. Season inside and out with the salt, pepper, and garlic. Refrigerate, uncovered, for at least 12 hours and up to 24 hours. Remove from the refrigerator 1 hour before you plan to start roasting.

Preheat the oven to 450°F/230°C/gas 8.

Put the ducks breast-side down on a rack set in a large roasting pan. Roast until the skin is browned, about 20 minutes. Reduce the oven temperature to 175°F/80°C, turn the ducks breast-side up, and roast until a thermometer inserted into the thickest part of a thigh (but not touching bone) registers 170°F/77°C, 4 to 6 hours. (Timing is not crucial; at that temperature the ducks will not overcook.)

While the ducks are roasting, in a small saucepan over medium-high heat, bring the balsamic vinegar to a boil. Cook until reduced by half, about 7 minutes.

To finish, raise the oven temperature to 500°F/260°C/gas 10. Remove the ducks from the oven and brush with the vinegar reduction. Roast until the skin of the duck breast is nicely browned all over and crisp, about 10 minutes longer.

Carve the ducks into serving pieces. Divide the duck pieces among dinner plates and serve.

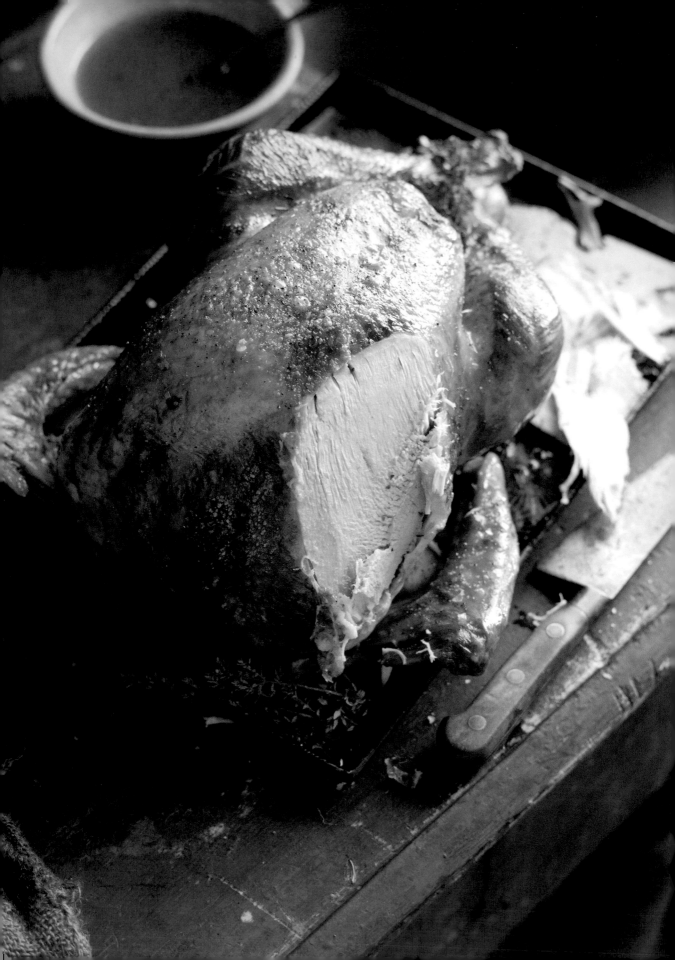

HOLIDAY
TURKEY

No roast desiccates more easily than a big-breasted turkey—it's a multidimensional anatomy problem. Turkey breast meat is finished cooking 10°F/5°C lower than the leg meat, so it is nearly impossible to get them perfectly cooked simultaneously. Miraculously, at least in its simplicity, the problem disappears when you slow-roast. By setting the oven temperature between the doneness temperatures of the breast and the leg, you cut your losses on both ends. The breast meat warms gently throughout, no section ever gets hotter than another, and the whole bird emerges moist and succulent.

CHILLING TIME: 12 to 24 hours **PREP TIME:** 5 min	**COOK TIME:** 14 hours or more	**STORE:** for up to 3 days, covered in the refrigerator. Reheat gently in a low oven.	*Makes* **15** *servings*

» 1 fresh turkey, about 15 lb/6.8 kg, preferably free-range

» Coarse sea salt and freshly ground black pepper

» 1 tbsp olive oil

» 1 qt/960 ml apple cider

» 2 tsp dried poultry seasoning

Remove the giblets from the turkey and discard (or save for another use). Rinse the turkey inside and out and pat dry with paper towels. Rub it all over with salt and pepper. Refrigerate, uncovered, for at least 12 hours and up to 24 hours. During that time, the surface of the turkey will become visibly dry and the skin will tighten; this encourages a nice crisp skin on the finished bird.

Remove the turkey from the refrigerator 1 hour before you plan to start roasting. Preheat the oven to 450°F/230°C/gas 8.

Put the turkey on a rack set in a large, flameproof roasting pan. Drizzle the olive oil over the top.

Roast for 1 hour. Reduce the oven temperature to 175°F/80°C. Pour the cider into the roasting pan and sprinkle the poultry seasoning in the liquid. Continue roasting until an instant-read thermometer inserted into the thickest part of a thigh (but not touching bone) registers 170°F/77°C, about 12 hours.

Transfer the turkey to a carving board, tent loosely with aluminum foil, and let rest for about 15 minutes (see Resting Slow-Cooked Meats box, page 33). Meanwhile, skim the fat from the surface of the liquid in the pan. Put the roasting pan over two burners and bring the pan drippings to a boil over high heat. Cook until the juices reduce and thicken slightly, enough to coat a spoon, about 10 minutes. Taste for seasoning. Carve the turkey and serve with cider pan juices.

TURKEY BREAST

This method is foolproof, and I am the fool to prove it. I have incinerated more than my share of turkey breasts with every conceivable roasting method, but I have never gone wrong by slow roasting. The reason is self-evident. By setting the oven thermostat at the same temperature I want the meat to be when it is done, overcooking becomes theoretically impossible (I say that because I suspect in practice, after several days of constant low heat, the overcooked scale would have to tip). But extreme slow roasting is so simple and requires so little labor, and the results are so exquisitely good, I fail to see why every other turkey-roasting method doesn't spontaneously combust in its presence.

CHILLING TIME: 12 to 24 hours PREP TIME: 5 minutes	COOKING TIME: about 8 hours	STORE: for up to 3 days, covered in the refrigerator. Reheat gently in a low oven.	*Makes about* **10** *servings*

» **1 whole bone-in turkey breast, 7 to 9 lb/3.2 to 4 kg**

» **¼ cup/30 g Homemade Italian Seasoning (page 90)**

» **1 large onion**

» **1 tbsp olive oil**

Pat the turkey breast dry with paper towels and rub it all over (including the bone side) with seasoning. Refrigerate uncovered for 12 to 24 hours. During that time, the surface of the turkey breast should become visibly dry and the skin will tighten.

Take the turkey out of the refrigerator 30 minutes to 1 hour before you want to start roasting. Set oven at 450°F/230°C/gas 8.

Peel the onion and trim its root end. Cut into big chunks, about 8, and put into a roasting pan in a tightly packed single layer. Put the turkey breast on the bed of onions, bone-side down. Drizzle the oil over the top.

Roast for 15 minutes. Reduce the oven temperature to 175°F/80°C and continue roasting until an instant-read thermometer inserted into the thickest part of the meat (without touching bone) reads 170°F/77°C, about 8 hours.

Rest at room temperature for 10 minutes before carving. Slow-roasted meats need far less resting time than those that are traditionally roasted.

SHORTCUT: HIGH-HEAT ROASTING

One big reason turkey breast meat has a tendency to dry out during cooking is that the actual fibers of the meat are delicate and easily broken, which belies suppleness and allows moisture to drain away. You can ensure moist results in two ways—super-high heat or super-low heat. Low-heat roasting (under 200°F/95°C), as in this recipe, never builds to an internal temperature hot enough to break the meat fibers, while high heat (over 425°F/220°C/gas 7) roasts the meat so quickly that only the surface gets hot enough to become dry and crispy. The low-heat method requires less vigilance and poses much less likelihood of drying out; but when you are in a hurry, you can speed things up with a judicious turn of the dial: rub the turkey breast with seasoning, let it stand at room temperature for an hour or so, and then roast at 450°F/230°C/gas 8 for about 1 hour, or until the internal temperature reaches 165°F/74°C.

SLOW-ROASTED PORK SHOULDER

WITH GARLIC-ROSEMARY BEANS

The shoulder of a pig is the most exercised muscle on the animal's body—it corresponds to the chuck in beef—and is therefore the most flavorful cut. It is highly striated with veins of fat that melt as the meat cooks, keeping it moist and succulent no matter how long it stays in the heat. This pork shoulder is roasted in a deep pot with tomatoes, white beans, and garlic cloves. As the meat cooks, the garlic breaks down into the sauce and infuses the beans with flavor, which are then served as a hearty side dish with the finished meat. One pot, two courses, practically no work.

CHILLING TIME: 4 to 24 hours **PREP TIME: 15** minutes	**COOKING TIME: 4½** to 6½ hours	**STORE:** for up 2 days, covered in the refrigerator. Reheat gently in a low oven.	*Makes* **6** *servings*

- » 2 tsp dried rosemary, crushed
- » 1 tsp dried sage
- » 1 tsp dried minced garlic
- » 1 tsp fine sea salt
- » ½ tsp freshly ground black pepper
- » 2 tbsp olive oil
- » 2½ lb/1.2 kg boneless pork shoulder, rolled and tied by the butcher
- » 1 medium yellow onion, diced
- » 2 cups/480 ml dry white wine such as Sauvignon Blanc
- » One 14½-oz/415-g can diced tomatoes, preferably fire-roasted, drained
- » Two 15-oz/430-g cans cannellini beans, drained and rinsed
- » ¼ cup/10 g coarsely chopped fresh rosemary
- » ¼ cup/10 g coarsely chopped fresh flat-leaf parsley
- » 2 garlic cloves, halved
- » 2 tbsp extra-virgin olive oil
- » 2 tbsp pine nuts, toasted (see Toasting Sesame Seeds or Pine Nuts box, page 39)

In a small bowl, stir together the dried rosemary, sage, garlic, and the salt and pepper. Rub the spice mixture all over the pork. Cover and refrigerate for at least 4 hours and up to overnight.

Preheat the oven to 175°F/80°C.

In a large Dutch oven over medium-high heat, heat the olive oil. Add the pork and sear until nicely browned on all sides, about 10 minutes total. Transfer to a plate.

Add the onion to the oil remaining in the pot, reduce the heat to medium, and sauté until browned, about 5 minutes. Add the wine, bring to a boil, and cook until reduced by half, about 10 minutes. Add the tomatoes and beans and return to a simmer, then remove the pot from the heat and set aside.

In a mini food processor, combine the fresh rosemary, the parsley, and the garlic clove halves and process until finely chopped. Add the extra-virgin olive oil and the pine nuts and pulse once or twice, just until combined. Stir half of the fresh herb mixture into the tomato-bean mixture and return the pork to the Dutch oven, along with any juices that accumulated on the plate. Roast until fork-tender, 4 to 6 hours.

Transfer the pork roast to a carving board, tent loosely with aluminum foil, and let rest for 5 to 10 minutes (see Resting Slow-Cooked Meats box, below). Meanwhile, return the Dutch oven to medium-high heat and bring the pan juices to a boil. Stir in the remaining fresh herb mixture. Using a slotted spoon, transfer the beans to a serving platter or divide among dinner plates. Snip the strings from the pork and, using a sharp chef's knife, carve across the grain on the diagonal into thin slices. Arrange the slices on the platter or plates, overlapping the beans. Spoon the tomatoes and juices in the pot over the pork and serve.

VARIATION: IN A SLOW COOKER

Follow the recipe, but transfer the pork to a 6-qt/5.7-l slow cooker rather than a plate after you finish browning it. After stirring half the herb mixture into the tomato-bean mixture, pour the bean mixture over the pork in the slow cooker and cook on low for 6 to 8 hours.

RESTING SLOW-COOKED MEATS

Slow-roasted meats need far less resting time (pretty much none) than those that are traditionally roasted. The reason for resting meat that has been roasted at a high temperature is to allow juices that have collected in the cooler center time to migrate back into the dryer (hotter) exterior sections after it comes out of the oven. Because slow-roasted meats are cooked evenly and at a temperature that keeps most of the juices in place, a resting period is largely unnecessary. A brief resting time does allow the meat to become a little firmer as it cools, making it easier to carve.

HONEY-GLAZED
∾ PIG ROAST ∾

A roast suckling pig is among the most extravagant of presentations, and though it may seem daunting, it is not difficult, especially when you slow-roast. After your pig is in the oven, slow cooking leaves you hours of stress-free time to stage a table or patio worthy of a glorious and memorable roast with golden, crackling skin and juicy meat.

The hardest part of a pig roast may be getting a pig, so be sure to plan ahead for your whole-hog event and talk to your favorite butcher about a special order (see Note). Barring access to a huge oven, the biggest pig most people can accommodate is about 20 lb/9 kg. The technique for tying a suckling pig for roasting is detailed below, but you can also ask the butcher to do it for you. To handle the techniques for this full-size roast with ease, you'll need long-handled tongs, a long-handled basting brush or mop, and a large carving board.

PREP TIME: 40 minutes	COOKING TIME: 4 to 5 hours	STORE: for up to 2 days, covered in the refrigerator. Reheat gently in a low oven.	*Makes* **10** *servings*

» ⅓ cup/75 ml honey

» 3 heads garlic, minced

» ¼ cup/55 g smoked sea salt

» ¼ cup/7 g smoked paprika

» 2 tbsp crushed dried rosemary

» 1 tbsp smoked black pepper

» ⅓ cup/75 ml canola oil, plus more for brushing

» 1 suckling pig, about 20 lb/9 kg

» 1 apple (optional)

FOR THE GLAZE:

» 2 cups/480 ml honey

» 2 cups/480 ml apple cider vinegar

» 1 cup/240 ml soy sauce

» ½ cup/120 ml ketchup

Preheat the oven to 200°F/95°C. Put an oven rack in the lowest position and wrap the top of the rack with a few sheets of heavy-duty aluminum foil. Position a second rack one level above.

In a bowl, stir together the honey, the garlic, salt, paprika, rosemary, and pepper. Add the oil and stir to blend well. Rub some of the honey mixture inside the cavity of the pig.

Position the legs under the pig. The front legs should be resting under the chin (the pig might come this way from the butcher) and the back legs should be set forward, bent from the hip, not the knee, so they extend along the belly. Tie the legs in place with several lengths of kitchen string. Position the ears so that they cover the pig's eyes and tie the ears with string to hold them in place. Rub the tied pig with the remaining spice mixture and slide the whole pig onto a length of heavy-duty foil just big enough to hold it. Stuff a ball of foil in the pig's mouth if you are planning to serve it with an apple in its mouth.

Put the pig, right-side up, on the higher rack and roast until the surface has begun to brown, about 2 hours.

While the pig is roasting, make the glaze: In a bowl, combine the honey, vinegar, soy sauce, and ketchup and stir to mix well. Pour half of the mixture into a serving bowl and set aside.

Snip the strings on the pig and remove. Brush the pig with half of the glaze, being sure to spread it evenly in all the nooks and crannies. Roast until an instant-read thermometer inserted into the thickest part of a thigh (but not touching bone) registers 165°F/74°C, 2 to 3 hours longer.

Transfer the pig to a carving board, tent loosely with aluminum foil, and let rest for 15 minutes (see Resting Slow-Cooked Meats box, page 33). Carve by cutting the pig into leg and shoulder sections and then cutting the meat from the bone in thin slices. Cut the ribs into 2-rib sections. Serve with the reserved glaze for dipping.

NOTE: *A suckling pig is not just a small pig; it is an infant, weighing under 25 lb/11.3 kg, and many supermarket meat departments will not order an item this specific. I suggest you look for a reputable Italian or Hispanic butcher, or order a frozen suckling pig from a top-quality online purveyor such as McReynolds Farms, www.mcreynoldsfarms.com.*

FORK-TENDER
❧ BEEF CHUCK ❧

WITH ONIONS, TOMATOES, AND OLIVES

This recipe is a showcase for how slow cooking works to concentrate flavors. The beef shoulder roast is first salted and refrigerated overnight in order to dry the surface, which will encourage the roast to brown deeply, a process of caramelizing that develops the rich roasted flavor. The sweet-savory vegetable accompaniments complement the salty-sweet beef, and are roasted on their own in advance to rid them of excess moisture and push them further into sublimity when they go into the roasting pan.

Once combined, the ingredients slow-cook together for several hours, punctuated by a splash of balsamic vinegar and briny Kalamata olives.

CHILLING TIME: 12 to 24 hours **PREP TIME: 10 minutes**	**COOKING TIME: about 3 hours** for the slow-roasted vegetables; 6 to 8 hours for the beef	**STORE:** for up to 3 days, covered in the refrigerator. Reheat gently in a low oven.	*Makes* **8** *servings*

» 1 boneless beef chuck roast, 3 to 4 lb/1.4 to 1.8 kg

» Coarse sea salt and freshly ground black pepper

» 12 large ripe plum tomatoes, cored and quartered

» 1 yellow onion, cut into 12 thin wedges

» 3 tbsp olive oil

» 1 tsp dried thyme

» 3 tbsp balsamic vinegar

» 12 pitted Kalamata olives, halved

» ¼ cup/10 g chopped fresh flat-leaf parsley

Rub the beef liberally with salt and pepper and set on a rack on a baking sheet. Refrigerate, uncovered, until the surface of the meat becomes visibly dry, at least 12 hours and up to 24 hours.

Preheat the oven to 200°F/95°C. Scatter the tomatoes and onion on a baking sheet and toss with 1 tbsp of the olive oil. Spread out in an even layer and season with salt and pepper. Roast until the vegetables are tender but still intact and pretty dry, about 3 hours. Set aside. (The vegetables can be roasted a day ahead of time.)

Remove the meat from the refrigerator. In a large Dutch oven over high heat, heat the remaining 2 tbsp olive oil until shimmering. Add the beef and sear until nicely browned, about 5 minutes per side. Remove from the heat and add the roasted tomatoes and onions, the thyme, vinegar, and olives to the pot. Cover and roast until the meat is very tender and is easily pierced with a fork, 6 to 8 hours.

Transfer the meat to a carving board, tent loosely with aluminum foil, and let rest for 10 minutes (see Resting Slow-Cooked Meats box, page 33). Meanwhile, skim the excess fat from the surface of the pan juices, bring to a vigorous boil over high heat, and cook until the liquid thickens slightly, about 4 minutes. Stir in the parsley.

Using a sharp chef's knife, carve the meat on the diagonal across the grain into thin slices. Serve immediately, with the tomatoes and onions as a pan sauce.

VARIATION: GRILLED ROAST BEEF

As an alternative way to serve, preheat the broiler while you let the meat cool almost to room temperature (still warm to the touch). Carve the meat into thick slices about ¾ in/2 cm thick. Brush the slices with a little neutral oil such as grapeseed and slip under the broiler to brown and crisp the surface of each slice, about 3 minutes per side. Serve with the tomato and onion sauce.

VARIATION: IN A SLOW COOKER

Follow the recipe, transferring the browned meat to a 6-qt/5.7-l slow cooker. Add the rest of the ingredients and cook on low for about 10 hours.

KOREAN
❧ BEEF RIBS ❧

Kalbi (also called *galbi*) are Korean short ribs cut from various sections of the ribs running from shoulder to loin on the steer. You'll be cutting the meat into thin butterflied strips for this recipe, so look for ribs with at least 1 in/2.5 cm of meat on the bones. Have your butcher remove the silver skin and fat from the ribs, then cut across the rib bones into 2-in/5-cm lengths. English-style ribs are cut between the bones, giving you a more rectangular piece of meat, which is better for roasting. Korean-style ribs are sliced across the bones, a cut better suited to braising or a quick grilling.

PREP TIME: 10 minutes	COOKING TIME: 4 to 5 hours	STORE: for up to 3 days, covered in the refrigerator. Reheat gently in a low oven.	*Makes* **4** TO **6** *servings*

» 1 small yellow onion, chopped

» 4 garlic cloves, chopped

» 1 tbsp peeled and finely chopped fresh ginger

» 1½ cups/360 ml unsweetened pineapple juice

» ½ cup/120 ml soy sauce

» ¼ cup/60 ml honey

» 1 tbsp molasses

» 1 tbsp toasted sesame oil

» 1 tbsp sake or dry white wine

» ½ tsp red pepper flakes

» 3 lb/1.4 kg English-style short ribs, cut into 2-in/5-cm lengths and butterflied (see Butterflying Short Ribs box, facing page)

FOR THE DIPPING SAUCE:

» ⅓ cup/75 ml soy sauce

» ⅓ cup/75 ml rice vinegar

» 1 tbsp sugar

» 2 tsp peeled and grated fresh ginger

» 1 tbsp sesame seeds, toasted (see Toasting Sesame Seeds or Pine Nuts box, facing page)

» 3 green onions, white and tender green parts, thinly sliced

» 8 to 12 medium romaine lettuce leaves, for wrapping

Preheat the oven to 200°F/95°C.

In a food processor, combine the onion, garlic, and 1 tbsp ginger and process to a purée. Add the pineapple juice, soy sauce, honey, molasses, sesame oil, sake, and red pepper flakes and process until mostly smooth. Pour into a roasting pan. Put the butterflied short ribs in the marinade and turn to coat. Roast until very tender, 4 to 5 hours.

While the meat is roasting, make the dipping sauce: In a small bowl, combine the soy sauce, vinegar, sugar, and ginger and stir until the sugar dissolves. Set aside.

Remove the pan from the oven and raise the oven temperature to 450°F/230°C/gas 8. Baste the meat well with the liquid in the pan. Return to the oven and roast until the surface of the meat is browned and the edges are crisping, 10 to 15 minutes longer, watching closely near the end to avoid burning.

Transfer the short ribs to a platter. Scatter the sesame seeds and green onions over the top. Arrange the lettuce leaves on a serving plate. To serve, invite diners to cut pieces of meat off the bone, wrap them in a lettuce leaf, and dip the packet into the sauce.

BUTTERFLYING SHORT RIBS

Position a rib section meaty-side up on a cutting board. Using a sharp, thin-bladed knife, cut through the longest side of the meat along the topside of bone, cutting the thickness in half and going almost but not all the way through to the other side. Open the two flaps so the meat lies flat like a book. Insert the knife into the meat near the bone, again halfway through the thickness, and make a second cut parallel to the board (you should have about ¼ in/6 mm of meat left on the bottom). Again cut almost but not all the way through the meat and then open up the flaps like a book. Make one or two more lengthwise cuts parallel to the board to open the meat flat. You should be left with a bone attached to a strip of meat about ¼ in/6 mm thick.

TOASTING SESAME SEEDS OR PINE NUTS

Because of their high oil content and diminutive size, it is easy to burn nuts and seeds in the process of toasting them. I like to use this safe method: Heat a cast-iron skillet over high heat for about 5 minutes. Remove the pan from the heat, add the nuts or seeds, and swirl in the hot pan until they are lightly browned and aromatic, about 1 minute.

PERFECT

 PRIME RIB

Although pretty much any beef rib roast is referred to informally as prime rib, less than 1 percent of the beef that is produced in the United States is actually officially graded "Prime," and most of that never reaches the retail market. In fact, the "prime" rib you purchase is usually "Choice" grade, which is fine; but if you know a butcher who deals in true Prime meat, this might be an occasion where you want the real thing. The combination of opulent marbling from Prime-level husbandry and lithe tenderness that is the hallmark of slow-roasted meats is hard to top.

Because a whole primal cut of beef rib is huge, weighing more that 40 lb/18 kg, a butcher is likely to ask you from which section you'd like your roast cut. End-cut rib roasts are more flavorful, fattier, and have an eye (the uninterrupted section of meat in the center of the roast) that is smaller and more striated with fat. Center-cut rib roast has a larger, leaner eye section, a milder flavor, and less fat. Choose whichever one suits your purposes best. Nothing beats the flavor of an end-cut rib, but if you want perfect lean slices that will wow your most discriminating guests, go for the center cut.

CHILLING TIME: 12 to 24 hours **PREP TIME: 10 minutes**	**COOKING TIME: 4½ to 6½ hours**	**STORE:** for up to 2 days, covered in the refrigerator. Reheat gently in a low oven.	*Makes* **8** TO **10** *servings*

» 6 garlic cloves, slivered

» One 4-rib standing beef rib roast, about 8 lb/3.6 kg

» 2 tsp coarse sea salt

» 1 tsp coarsely ground black pepper

Slip the garlic slivers between the meat and fat on the top of the roast, and between the meat and bones on the bottom. Season the roast all over with the salt and pepper and refrigerate, uncovered, until the surface is visibly dry, at least 12 hours and up to 24 hours. Remove from the refrigerator 1 hour before you plan to start roasting.

Preheat the oven to 550°F/290°C.

Place the beef in a large roasting pan, fat-side up, and roast for about 20 minutes, or until the surface is starting to brown. Reduce the oven temperature to 150°F/65°C. (If your thermostat doesn't go that low, set it at its lowest setting, often 175°F/80°C.) Roast until an instant-read thermometer inserted into the center of the meat (but not touching bone) registers 135°F/57°C, 4 to 6 hours.

Transfer the meat to a carving board, tent loosely with aluminum foil, and let rest for 15 minutes (see Resting Slow-Cooked Meats box, page 33).

CONTINUED

Stand the rested roast upright, and use a sharp carving knife to cut between the bones and the meat. Detatch the bones. Hold the roast steady with a carving fork or your hand, and slice the meat into thin, even slices.

Divide the slices among dinner plates and serve immediately.

NOTE: *Beef rib roasts are sold by the number of ribs in the roast, with each rib weighing about 2 pounds, and feeding 2 people (a pound of bone-in rib yields less than 1 pound of edible meat).*

VARIATION: RIB ROAST WITH GARLIC JUS

After transferring the finished roast to a carving board, pour the pan drippings into a gravy separator. Spoon 2 tbsp of the fat from the surface into a saucepan and heat over medium-high heat. Add 2 garlic cloves, minced, to the fat and cook until aromatic, about 30 seconds. Add the meat juices from the separator, leaving the remaining fat behind. Add 1 cup/240 ml dry red wine and bring to a boil. Add 1 cup/240 ml good-quality low-sodium beef broth, return to a boil, and cook until reduced by half, about 10 minutes. Season with salt and pepper. Stir in 1 tbsp chopped fresh flat-leaf parsley. Carve the beef and serve with the jus.

VARIATION: RIB ROAST WITH PORT WINE GLAZE

After transferring the finished roast to a carving board, spoon the fat out of the pan and discard, or pour all of the pan drippings into a gravy separator and pour the meat juices back into the roasting pan, leaving the fat behind. Add a sprig of fresh rosemary and 2 cups/480 ml port wine to the pan. Place over medium-high heat (make sure you have a flameproof roasting pan) and boil until reduced by half, about 10 minutes. Discard the rosemary. Carve the beef and serve with the sauce.

BONELESS VERSUS BONE-IN MEATS

Bones slow down the movement of heat through meat, which is why boneless chicken and turkey roast so much more quickly than bone-in birds. It's also why they dry out. Whenever you roast delicately textured meats, like poultry breast, pork, lamb, veal, or fish, slowing down heat transference, either by lowering the oven temperature or choosing cuts on the bone for roasting, reduces the chance that the meat fibers will get hot enough to break down and dry out. Slow cooking bone-in meats and fish doubles the delicious benefits.

HERBED LEG OF LAMB

❧ WITH BRANDY GLAZE ❧

Boneless leg of lamb has become so commonplace, it can be a trial finding a whole leg on the bone. This is a shame, because meat roasted on the bone is far superior in flavor and juiciness. I encourage you to make the effort to track down a bone-in roast, especially for the slow-cooking method, which renders the rich meat meltingly "tender to the bone."

You may find it off-putting to face carving a whole leg of lamb, but it's arguably easier than carving a turkey, and basic knife skills will serve you fine. You can carve on the bone, or remove the bone before you slice, which is best done in the kitchen; then you can show off the beautiful, aromatic glazed roast at the table, carving it into thin slices.

CHILLING TIME: 12 to 24 hours	COOKING TIME: 4½ to 6½ hours	STORE: for up to 2 days, covered in the refrigerator. Reheat gently in a low oven.	*Makes* **6** TO **8** *servings*
PREP TIME: 5 minutes			

» ½ cup/55 g Homemade Italian Seasoning (page 90)

» 1 whole bone-in leg of lamb, 5 to 6 lb/2.3 to 2.7 kg, surface fat trimmed to ¼ in/6 mm

» ¼ cup/60 ml walnut oil or olive oil

» ½ cup/120 ml brandy

Scatter the seasoning all over the lamb and pat with your fingers to help it adhere. Set the seasoned lamb on a rack in a roasting pan and refrigerate for at least 12 hours or up to 24 hours.

Remove the lamb from the refrigerator to take the chill off while you preheat the oven to 550°F/290°C. In a small bowl, stir together the oil and brandy to make a glaze.

Put the lamb in the oven and roast until starting to brown, about 20 minutes. Brush the lamb all over with the glaze. Reduce the oven temperature to 150°F/65°C. (If your thermostat doesn't go that low, set it at its lowest setting, often 175°F/80°C.) Roast, brushing the lamb with more of the glaze every hour, until an instant-read thermometer inserted into the center of the meat (but not touching bone) registers 135°F/57°C, 4 to 6 hours, depending on oven temperature. Transfer the lamb to a carving board, tent loosely with aluminum foil, and let rest for 15 minutes (see Resting Slow-Cooked Meats box, page 33).

You can remove the bone in the kitchen and then carve the roast into slices at the table, if you like. To remove the bone, put the lamb on its side and make a slit with a slender knife along the bone from one end to the other. Continue working your knife around the bone until it can be lifted out. Because slow-roasted meat is so tender, it is not difficult to separate it from the bone.

To carve the leg on the bone, put the lamb on its side. Starting on the outside, cut thin lengthwise slices until you reach the bone. Turn the leg onto the cut side. Starting at the thicker end, cut thin crosswise slices. You won't hit bone for the first few slices. When you do hit bone, continue to slice through the meat above the bone until you get to the end of the leg. Separate the slices from the bone by making a long, horizontal cut down the length of the bone, running the knife blade along the bone and following the contour.

Arrange the slices on a platter or plates and serve.

CHAPTER 2

—

· SLOW ·

BAKING

Baking and roasting both take place in an oven, and
I don't know if the differences are much more than semantic, but to me roasts
are big hunks of meat. I think of a whole haunch of venison roasting on a spit over a
roaring fire. Baked things are smaller, more delicate, and more contained. Where
roasts need to be exposed to the open air of the oven, baked foods call for nestling in
baking dishes. They might be layered with a sauce, simmered in gravy, or warmed
in a covered casserole. All of which gives baked items the benefit of more moisture,
both added and retained. Of course there are exceptions that blur these distinctions.
Roasted vegetables are cut in small pieces, like baked items, but they are never protected by a sauce, allowing them to brown and caramelize. A ham is usually said to be
baked even though it is shaped like a large roast, probably because it is precured and
therefore only needs to be warmed, rather than cooked through in the oven.

By lowering the oven temperature, evaporation is lessened, preserving more of
the moisture and making slow-baked foods more succulent. Baking meat sauce for
pasta rather than simmering it on a stove top slows down the cooking and evaporation, and the meat gets more time to soften and integrate into the sauce. Slow-baked
meatloaf is creamier and moister than meatloaf cooked at higher temperatures, and
slow-baked fish never gets hot enough to lose its juices.

Baking watery vegetables like tomatoes achieves the same flavor-boosting
effect but from opposite results. Baking tomatoes dries them out, which is exactly
what you want to have happen. The moisture in tomatoes and other soft vegetables
is mostly water, so by releasing that water and evaporating it away, you concentrate
the natural flavor of the produce. Oven-dried tomatoes look shriveled, but they
embody the very essence of tomato.

MAC AND CHEESE

This mac and cheese is a cinch. You don't precook the noodles and you don't make a sauce. Everything just gets tossed in a casserole dish and baked. Because it bakes slowly in a low oven set to the doneness temperature for the casserole, it is impossible to overcook. Throw it together in the morning, enjoy the smell of simmering cheese sauce all day, and dig in that night. It's that easy.

PREP TIME: 10 minutes	**COOKING TIME:** 6 to 8 hours	**STORE:** for up to 4 days, covered in the refrigerator. Reheat gently in a low oven.	*Makes* **6** *servings*

» **2 tbsp unsalted butter, melted**

» **12 oz/340 g dried elbow macaroni**

» **1 lb/455 g sharp Cheddar cheese, shredded**

» **4 cups/960 ml milk**

» **2 tsp brown mustard**

» **1½ tsp fine sea salt**

» **1 tsp freshly ground black pepper**

» **1 cup/55 g fresh bread crumbs**

» **½ tsp dried thyme**

Preheat the oven to 200°F/95°C.

Grease the inside of a 2-qt/2-l casserole with 1 or 2 tsp of the melted butter. Make four layers of macaroni alternating with three layers of shredded cheese in the prepared casserole dish.

In a bowl, whisk together the milk, mustard, salt, and pepper and pour into the casserole. Poke down any macaroni that aren't submerged. Sprinkle evenly with the bread crumbs and thyme, and drizzle the remaining melted butter over the top. Cover with aluminum foil and bake until the macaroni is tender and the cheese is melted, 6 to 8 hours.

Raise the oven temperature to 450°F/230°C/gas 8. Remove the foil and bake until the top of the casserole is crisp and brown, about 15 minutes longer. Serve immediately.

OVEN-DRIED TOMATOES

Tomatoes are full of flavor. They're also full of water. Getting rid of the water concentrates and intensifies the flavor, but most of the time even slow-roasted tomatoes collapse by the time full flavor develops—think fresh tomatoes cooking down into sauce. A treat, to be sure, but a different way of experiencing the tomato.

As an alternative, tomatoes baked extremely slowly in the oven have all the concentrated flavor of a long-simmered tomato sauce, but each tomato retains its shape, creating colorful, chewy (and pretty) little bombs of tomato flavor at its best. The trick is low heat, slow cooking—and keeping your hands off! Low heat at the beginning of cooking activates an enzyme in the vegetable's cell walls that prevents the cells from weakening; if you don't stir or otherwise disturb, the fruit remains intact even over hours of cooking. Serve as a side dish, toss with pasta, or use in stews and braises such as Lamb Shanks Slow-Baked (page 74).

PREP TIME: 10 minutes	**COOKING TIME:** about 6 hours	**STORE:** for up to 5 days, covered in the refrigerator.	*Makes* **10** TO **12** *servings*

» 3 lb/1.4 kg ripe plum tomatoes, cored and halved lengthwise

» 6 garlic cloves, finely chopped

» ¼ cup/60 ml olive oil

» 2 tsp whole crystal sea salt, oversize crystals crushed between your fingers

» 1 tsp freshly ground black pepper

Preheat the oven to 200°F/95°C.

Combine the tomatoes, garlic, olive oil, salt, and pepper on a baking sheet and toss to mix and coat well. Shake the pan to make everything slide into a single layer.

Roast until the tomatoes have shrunk by about half and no longer appear wet on their surface, about 6 hours. There's no need to peek or stir during cooking, and no harm done if they roast for an extra hour or so.

Remove from the oven and let cool on the pan for 15 minutes to firm up. Scrape off the pan using a rubber spatula or wooden spoon and use within 5 days.

VARIATION: IN A SLOW COOKER

You can slow-roast tomatoes in a 6-qt/5.7-l slow cooker on low for 4 to 6 hours. Cover the crockery with a folded flat-weave kitchen towel before putting on the lid to wick away excess moisture.

CARROTS
SLOW-BAKED
ON COFFEE BEANS

It appeared mysteriously spartan on the menu at Coi, Daniel Patterson's ashram for food in San Francisco's North Beach: "Carrots/Coffee." What did it mean? It turned out to be genius—sweet, smoky, and earthy genius. Pencil-thin carrots are baked on a bed of coffee beans that warm gently, releasing their oils. This unexpected dish celebrates all the advantages of slow cooking: the coffee fumes gradually infuse the vegetables, creating an ephemeral sensation of something roasted that one can identify as "coffee" only after the tongue whispers to the brain.

PREP TIME: 10 minutes	COOKING TIME: 2 to 3 hours	STORE: for up to 3 days, covered in the refrigerator. Reheat gently in a low oven.	Makes **4** servings

» 1 lb/455 g thin carrots (no thicker than ½ in/12 mm in diameter), peeled

» 1 tsp olive oil

» 1 small garlic clove, minced

» Coarse sea salt and coarsely ground black pepper

» 1 cup/90 g medium-roast coffee beans, preferably decaf

Preheat the oven to 225°F/110°C/gas ¼. Place a cast-iron skillet over medium heat to heat for about 5 minutes.

In a large bowl, combine the carrots, olive oil, and garlic and toss until the carrots are slicked with oil and the garlic bits are distributed evenly. Season with salt and pepper; set aside.

Add the coffee beans to the hot skillet and remove from heat. Shake until the coffee is aromatic and the beans look a bit oily, about 3 minutes. Scatter the carrots over the beans in a single layer and cover the pan with a lid or a sheet of heavy-duty aluminum foil. Bake until the carrots are fork-tender and infused with coffee oil, 2 to 3 hours.

Lift the carrots from the bed of coffee beans and serve immediately. Discard the coffee.

SLOW-BAKED WHOLE PUMPKIN

STUFFED WITH PUMPKIN-SEED RISOTTO

Cinderella's fairy godmother sure was crafty; turning that pumpkin into a coach was one nifty piece of handwork. This recipe would give her a run for the money, or the glass slipper: a pumpkin filled with risotto, white beans, a savory broth, and three cheeses—a perfect fit.

Extravagant-seeming, with plump risotto rice and a whole sweet pumpkin, this is a comforting side dish that's simple to assemble and low-maintenance, slow cooking–style, and can also be served as a show-stopping vegetarian main dish. Present the pumpkin at the table intact; when you lift the lid, you should hear some ooooohs and ahhhhs.

When selecting a pumpkin for this dish, choose one that is wide and squat rather than round; a short, wide squash will cook through more evenly than one that is tall or shaped like a basketball.

PREP TIME: 40 minutes	**COOKING TIME:** 4 to 5 hours, plus 10 minutes for precooking the rice	**STORE:** for up to 2 days, covered in refrigerator. Reheat gently in a low oven.	*Makes* **12** *servings*

» 2 tbsp olive oil

» 1 large Spanish onion, finely chopped

» 4 garlic cloves, minced

» Sea salt and freshly ground black pepper

» 4 cups/960 ml good-quality low-sodium vegetable broth

» 1½ cup/315 g Arborio or Carnaroli rice

» Two 15-oz/430-g cans small white beans such as navy beans or pea beans, rinsed and drained

» 1 cup/225 g Mexican *crema* or mascarpone cheese

» 1 cup/240 ml heavy (whipping) cream

» ¾ cup/100 g roasted pumpkin seeds

» 1 cup/115 g freshly grated Parmesan cheese, preferably Parmigiano-Reggiano

» 3 tbsp toasted (dark) sesame oil

Heat the olive oil in a large skillet over medium-high heat. Add the onion and sauté until tender, about 3 minutes. Add the garlic and cook until aromatic, about 30 seconds. Season with salt and pepper; set aside.

Bring the broth to a boil in a large saucepan over high heat. Reduce the heat to medium and add a big pinch of salt and the rice. Return to a boil and cook until the rice is just starting to turn tender, about 10 minutes. In a bowl, combine the rice with the beans, *crema*, cream, pumpkin seeds, Parmesan, sesame oil, and nutmeg. Taste and adjust the seasoning with salt and pepper; set aside.

Preheat the oven to 300°F/150°C/gas 2.

Cut around the stem of the pumpkin to create a lid, and remove. Clean the interior cavity of seeds and pulp in the same way you would if you were preparing to carve it as a jack-o'-lantern. Using a big spoon, scrape the flesh from the inside of the top half of the pumpkin, reducing its thickness by about half. Allow the scraped flesh to collect on the bottom, which will help the whole pumpkin roast more evenly. Cut a slice from the interior of the pumpkin's lid, reducing its thickness by half, and place the slice on the bottom of the pumpkin as well.

- » **A generous grating freshly grated nutmeg**
- » **1 large pumpkin, about 12 lb/ 5.5 kg, with a stem**
- » **8 oz/225 g fontina cheese, shredded**

Fold a sheet of heavy-duty aluminum foil into fourths to make a square large enough to cradle the bottom of the pumpkin, and set the pumpkin on top. Season the interior of the pumpkin with salt and pepper and scatter half of the fontina over the bottom. Fill the pumpkin with the rice and bean mixture. Top with the remaining fontina. Replace the lid on the pumpkin and wrap the whole thing, including the folded foil base, in two layers of heavy-duty foil. Bake until the pumpkin is soft (poke gently with your finger or a wooden spoon to test it), 4 to 5 hours.

Remove the pumpkin from the oven and transfer to a large platter. Let rest for 10 minutes. Remove the foil from the top and sides of the pumpkin, tearing it around the base so that the pumpkin is still resting on foil but the excess foil doesn't show. Remove the lid and serve, scooping some of the soft pumpkin flesh with each ladleful of risotto.

SLOW-BAKED BEETS

WITH ORANGE GREMOLATA

Beets are sweet! But you may have never known this, if you've only had them boiled. The thing is, sugar is water-soluble—so boiling beets largely washes the sweetness away, leaving behind little more than the flavor of dirt. Quite on the other hand, if you bake beets, the sugar concentrates, the dense fiber softens, and they become lush and meaty. When slow-baked, the sugars don't caramelize the way they do at higher roasting temperatures, yielding sweetness in equal measure, but one that is as clean and refined as sugar.

In this recipe, I usurped *gremolata*, the classic garnish for *osso buco Milanese*, for the topping.

PREP TIME: 5 minutes	COOKING TIME: about 6½ hours	STORE: for up to 3 days, covered in the refrigerator. Reheat gently in a saucepan over low heat.	*Makes* **6** *servings*

» 2 lb/910 red beets (about 8 medium), scrubbed, greens and long roots trimmed

» 2 tbsp olive oil

FOR THE *GREMOLATA*:

» ¼ cup/35 g hazelnuts

» Finely grated zest and juice of 1 orange

» ½ garlic clove, coarsely chopped

» 1 tbsp olive oil

» 1 tbsp chopped fresh flat-leaf parsley

» Sea salt and freshly ground black pepper

Preheat the oven to 225°F/110°C/gas ¼.

Put the beets on a large sheet of heavy-duty aluminum foil and drizzle with 1 tbsp of the olive oil. Wrap the foil around the beets and bake until fork-tender, about 6 hours.

While the beets are cooking, prepare the *gremolata*: Heat a heavy skillet over high heat for 3 minutes. Add the hazelnuts and stir for 30 seconds. Remove from the heat and keep stirring until the nuts are toasted. Dump the nuts out of the pan onto a kitchen towel. Fold the towel around the nuts and rub them vigorously to remove their papery skins. Pick up the nuts, leaving the flakes of skin behind in the towel. Chop the nuts finely in a food processor (pulse carefully, or you may end up with nut butter) or with a knife. In a small bowl, mix the nuts, orange zest and juice, garlic, olive oil, and parsley, and season with salt and pepper.

When the beets are done, remove from the oven and let cool until cool enough to handle, about 15 minutes. Unwrap the foil and peel the beets with a small knife and by rubbing with your fingers. Cut each beet into eight wedges.

Heat the remaining 1 tbsp olive oil in a skillet or saucepan over medium heat. Add the beets and stir until heated through, about 2 minutes. Toss with the *gremolata* and serve.

PARSNIPS BAKED

IN SPICED YOGURT

Neglected and maligned, parsnips have a PR problem. Along with turnips, they are often included in the ubiquitous bag of vegetables known as "soup blend" and perhaps thus get lumped in the minds of cooks with blander roots; they rarely get to shine on their own. It's a shame, because parsnips are truly delicious. Sweeter than carrots and as meaty as beets, parsnips make for easy, pleasing side dishes. Think of throwing together this slow-cooked version on a crisp day in late fall, when the parsnips left in the ground during the frosty nights become extra sweet. I hope this recipe, redolent with curry-like spices, resurrects parsnips in your cooking repertoire. The yogurt transforms into soft, pleasantly chewy curds as it cooks, delivering wonderful flavor in a texture like cottage cheese.

PREP TIME: 20 minutes	**COOKING TIME:** 2½ to 3½ hours	**STORE:** for up to 3 days, covered in refrigerator. Reheat gently over low heat.	*Makes* **4** *servings*

» 1 lb/455 g parsnips, peeled and cut into 1-in/2.5-cm pieces

» 1 to 2 tbsp canola oil

» 1 yellow onion, peeled and thinly sliced

» One 1-in/2.5-cm piece fresh ginger, peeled and cut into matchsticks

» 1 cinnamon stick, broken into 2 to 4 pieces (a few taps with a hammer works well)

» 1 tsp ground coriander

» 1 tsp ground cumin

» ½ tsp ground cardamom

» Pinch of ground cloves

» Sea salt and freshly ground black pepper

» 1 cup/240 ml yogurt

» 2 tbsp chopped fresh cilantro

Preheat the oven to 275°F/135°C/gas 1.

Bring a small saucepan of water to a boil over high heat. Add the parsnips and simmer until barely tender, about 10 minutes; drain.

Meanwhile, in a large cast-iron skillet over medium-low heat, heat just enough oil to coat the bottom of the pan. Add the onion, ginger, and cinnamon and cook until the onion softens, about 5 minutes. Add the ground spices and cook until the mixture is very fragrant, about 2 minutes. Add more oil if the mixture looks dry. Add the drained parsnips and season liberally with salt and pepper. Remove from the heat.

Stir in the yogurt. Cover with a lid or a sheet of heavy-duty aluminum foil and bake for 2 to 3 hours, until the yogurt is thick (it will curdle a little, resembling cottage cheese) and the vegetables are very soft and fragrant. Garnish with the cilantro and serve.

SALMON

WITH SPICED RED LENTILS AND BACON

Fish is easily overcooked, which makes it a strong candidate for slow cooking and an easy night's work for the cook—unless of course you complicate matters by throwing something tricky into the mix. I love a culinary dare. Rich fish like salmon and mackerel are delicious served with beans, but the two cook at such different rates, they typically can't be cooked together. By using red lentils, which are the softest of dried beans, and a forgiving fatty fish, like farm-raised salmon, I found I could trim the difference to about 10 minutes. A brief simmering of the lentils on their own does it; then the salmon is added and everything slow-bakes together in a low oven.

This is a heady, aromatic, elegant one-pot meal. A rainbow of spices elevates this homey dish to a sure thing for a splash at a dinner party—and stirring them together may be the most labor-intensive part of the simple slow-cooking method.

| **PREP TIME:** 30 minutes | **COOKING TIME:** about 1½ hours | **STORE:** for up to 1 day, covered in the refrigerator. Reheat gently in a low oven. | *Makes* **4** *servings* |

FOR THE SPICE RUB:

- » 2 tsp ground coriander
- » 1 tsp ground cumin
- » 1 tsp ground turmeric
- » ½ tsp sweet paprika
- » ¼ tsp ground cinnamon
- » ⅛ tsp cayenne pepper
- » 1 tsp coarse sea salt
- » ½ tsp freshly ground black pepper

- » 1½ lb/680 g farm-raised salmon fillet, in 1 large piece about 1½ in/4 cm thick, skin removed (see Skinning a Fish Fillet box, page 59)
- » 2 bacon strips
- » 1 medium yellow onion, finely chopped
- » 2 garlic cloves, minced
- » 1 cup/180 g red lentils
- » ½ cup/120 ml canned diced tomatoes, with juice
- » 2 cups/480 ml good-quality low-sodium chicken or vegetable broth
- » 2 tbsp chopped fresh cilantro

To make the spice rub: In a bowl, mix together all the ingredients.

Rub 2 tsp of the mixture into the flesh of the salmon fillet; set aside for 30 minutes. Preheat the oven to 200°F/95°C.

In a large cast-iron skillet, cook the bacon over medium heat until crisp and the bottom of the pan is coated with the rendered fat, 5 to 8 minutes. Transfer the bacon to paper towels to drain, then cut into small pieces.

Put the skillet over high heat. When the fat is hot, gently put the salmon in the pan, pinker-side down. (One side of a salmon fillet will be bright pink and the other side will have a strip of dark flesh running down the center. The bright pink side is the one you want to brown.) Sear until nicely browned on the bottom, about 3 minutes. Using two large spatulas, carefully transfer the salmon to a sheet of heavy-duty aluminum foil, browned-side up.

Add the onion to the fat in the pan and sauté over medium-high heat until translucent, about two minutes. Add the garlic and the remaining spice blend and stir until aromatic, about 20 seconds. Stir in the lentils, tomatoes with their juice, and broth and simmer for 10 minutes.

CONTINUED

Using the foil as a kind of large spatula, carefully slide the salmon onto the lentils. Cover the skillet with a lid or a clean sheet of heavy foil and bake until the thickest part of the fish flakes to gentle pressure and the lentils are tender, about 1 hour.

Garnish with the chopped cilantro and slip onto a large platter or serve directly from the pan.

VARIATION: IN A SLOW COOKER

Follow the directions in the recipe. Use a sheet of heavy-duty aluminum foil 2 ft/60 cm long for resting the browned salmon. Scrape the lentil mixture into a 5- to 6-qt/4.5- to 5.7-l, oval-shaped slow cooker. Using the foil as a plate, set the salmon, still on the foil, on top of the lentils. Drape the long ends of the foil up the sides and over the edges of the slow-cooker crock, like handles. Cover and cook on low for 2 hours. Lift the salmon on its foil sling. Mound the lentils on a serving platter and carefully slide the salmon from the foil onto the bed of lentils. Garnish with the chopped cilantro and serve.

SKINNING A FISH FILLET

To remove the skin from a fish fillet, place the fillet skin-side down on a cutting board, long side facing you. Have the tail end closest to your knife-holding hand. Slip a thin-bladed boning knife between the skin and the flesh of the tail end of the fillet. Holding your knife blade parallel to the board and angled slightly toward the skin, run the blade between skin and the fish flesh, sawing gently to strip the skin from the flesh. Try to leave as little flesh on the skin as possible.

SEAFOOD
❧ CASSOULET ❧

Unlike classic versions loaded with sausage, beans, and confit, this enlightened version of cassoulet doesn't weigh you down. Hearty it is, but leaden, never. The difference comes from switching out most of the meat for fruits of the sea. The flavors are lighter and brighter, and the combination of earthy beans and briny seafood reinvents surf 'n' turf deliciously. The slow-cooking technique allows the flavors to develop and deepen for hours without danger of turning the shellfish rubbery.

PREP TIME: 20 minutes, plus 1 hour to overnight (depending on how you soak the beans)	**COOKING TIME:** 4 to 5 hours	**STORE:** for up to 2 days, covered in the refrigerator. Reheat gently in a low oven.	*Makes* **6** *servings*

» 1 lb/455 g white navy beans

» 1 lb/455 g andouille sausage

» 1 tbsp ground coriander

» 2 tsp ground cumin

» 1 tsp ground ginger

» 1 tsp dry mustard

» 4 fresh dill sprigs

» 4 fresh flat-leaf parsley sprigs

» ¼ cup/60 ml olive oil

» 1 large leek, white part only, cleaned and thinly sliced

» 4 garlic cloves, thinly sliced

» Sea salt and freshly ground black pepper

» ½ cup/120 ml dry white wine

» 12 cherrystone clams, scrubbed

» 2 lb/910 g mussels, scrubbed and debearded

» 1 lemon, halved and seeded

» 8 oz/225 g extra-large (21–25 count) shrimp, peeled and deveined

» 8 oz/225 g sea scallops, rinsed and patted dry

Pick over the beans for stones or grit. Rinse in a colander and drain well. Put the beans in a bowl and add water to cover by at least 3 in/7.5 cm. Let soak for at least 4 hours or overnight, then drain. Alternatively, put the beans in a saucepan, add water to cover by at least 3 in/7.5 cm, and bring to a boil. Boil for 3 minutes, then remove from the heat and let the beans soak for 1 hour. Drain.

In a large saucepan, bring 2 qt/2 l water to a boil. Add the beans, sausage, coriander, cumin, ginger, and mustard and stir. Tie the dill and parsley sprigs into a bouquet garni with kitchen string and toss into the pot. Bring to a boil over high heat, then reduce the heat to medium and simmer until the beans are tender, about 55 minutes.

Meanwhile in a large Dutch oven, heat the olive oil over medium heat. Add the leek and sauté for 1 minute. Add the garlic and cook for 1 minute more. Season with salt and pepper, then add the wine and the clams, discarding any clams that do not close to the touch. Cover and steam until the shells open, about 10 minutes. (Discard any clams that fail to open.) Transfer the clams to a bowl and discard the shells. Pour any liquid from the clam shells back into the pot.

Add the mussels, cover, and steam until the shells open, about 3 minutes. (Discard any mussels that fail to open.) Transfer the mussels to the bowl with the clams and discard the shells. Using a slotted spoon, transfer the leeks and garlic from the seafood cooking liquid to a small bowl. Strain the remaining liquid through a coffee filter into the bowl with the leeks to remove any grit from the shellfish. Set aside. Wipe the Dutch oven clean and set aside.

When the beans are done cooking, drain the cooking liquid into a smaller saucepan. Set the pan with the beans aside. Using tongs, transfer the sausage to a cutting board and cut into ¾-in/2-cm slices. Set aside. Bring the bean-cooking liquid to a boil over high heat and cook until reduced to about 1 cup/240 ml, about 5 minutes. Add the strained seafood cooking liquid along with the leeks and garlic to the bean-cooking liquid, then pour the mixture into the cooked beans. Squeeze the juice from the lemon halves into the saucepan and stir well.

Preheat the oven to 175°F/80°C.

To assemble, make a layer of one-third of the beans in the bottom of the Dutch oven. Follow with half of the clams, mussels, shrimp, scallops, and sausage; another one-third of the beans; the remaining seafood and sausage; and the rest of the beans, in that order. Cover and bake until the casserole is crusty on top and bubbling around the edges, 3 to 4 hours. Serve immediately.

OSSO BUCO

WITH APPLES AND BOURBON

Osso buco, a slow-cooked regional specialty from Milan, is named quite literally—*osso* is the Italian word for "bone," and *buco* means "hole," the combination referring to the donut shape of a cross-section of veal shank bone, plus the marrow hidden in its core.

During the cooking of osso buco, the shank transforms so thoroughly, it's almost magical. Not only does the naturally tough and sinewy meat become moist and tender, but the dense, pasty marrow turns custardy and luscious. At the same time, the membranes and cartilage surrounding the bone and connecting the meat melt into the sauce, making it exceptionally rich and flavorful. The whole process is ideally suited to the longest, slowest cooking technique possible. For a final gilding, when the shanks are done, the simmering liquid has become a syrupy glaze with the exquisite flavors of a finely crafted consommé.

PREP TIME: 15 minutes	**COOKING TIME:** 7½ to 10½ hours	**STORE:** for up to 3 days, covered in the refrigerator. Reheat gently in a low oven.	*Makes* **4** *servings*

» **4 pieces veal shank, each about 14 oz/400 g and 2 in/5 cm thick**

» **All-purpose flour for dredging**

» **Coarse sea salt and freshly ground black pepper**

» **2 tbsp vegetable oil**

» **2 tbsp unsalted butter**

» **2 leeks, white parts only, chopped**

» **2 celery stalks, peeled and finely diced**

» **2 garlic cloves, minced**

» **¼ cup/60 ml bourbon**

» **1 cup/240 ml good-quality low-sodium beef broth**

» **½ cup/120 ml apple cider**

» **2 tsp dried rosemary, crumbled**

» **1 tsp dried thyme**

» **Finely grated zest of ½ orange**

» **1 bay leaf**

» **2 large tart apples such as Granny Smith, peeled, cored, and cut into chunks**

» **½ cup/120 ml heavy cream**

Preheat the oven to 200°F/95°C.

Tie each piece of veal shank securely around its perimeter with kitchen twine.

Season the flour with salt and pepper on a sheet of aluminum foil. In a large Dutch oven, heat the oil over high heat. When the oil is hot, add the shanks and sear, turning once, until browned nicely on the top and bottom, about 10 minutes total. Transfer to a plate.

Reduce the heat to medium and add the butter. When the butter is melted, add the leeks, celery, and garlic and sauté until the leeks are just starting to soften, about 5 minutes. Return the shanks to the pan along with any juices that accumulated on the plate. Add the bourbon and bring to a boil. Add the broth, cider, rosemary, thyme, orange zest, and bay leaf. Return to a simmer, then remove from the heat. Cover and bake until the meat is fork-tender and the marrow has shrunk inside the bone, at least 5 hours (but there is no harm in going longer, up to 8 hours). Add the apples and bake until the apples are soft, about 2 hours longer.

CONTINUED

Skim the fat from the surface of the cooking liquid and add the cream. Taste and adjust the seasoning with salt and pepper. Carefully transfer the shanks to a platter, untying each one as you do. Spoon the sauce over the shanks and serve.

VARIATION: IN A SLOW COOKER
Put the shanks in a 6-qt/5.7-l slow cooker after browning. Make the sauce as described and add to the cooker. Lay the apples on top. Cover and cook for 3 to 4 hours on high or 6 to 8 hours on low. Finish with the cream and serve.

HANGER STEAK

SLOW-BAKED IN ITS OWN DEMI-GLACE

Demi-glace, the wine-fortified clear meat broth that epitomizes the classic French kitchen, takes hours to produce properly. Fortunately, when you're slow cooking, time is exactly what you've got. As the meat, spices, vegetables, and wine simmer together, their flavors gradually mingle and bloom, effortlessly creating the depth of flavor and silken texture that is the hallmark of classic demi-glace.

Hanger steak is also known as "butcher's steak" because butchers typically kept this cut for themselves. It is a small, oddly shaped steak, usually weighing about 1 lb/455 g.

PREP TIME: 10 minutes	**COOKING TIME:** about 6½ hours	**STORE:** Best served immediately.	*Makes* **4** *servings*

» ¼ cup/30 g all-purpose flour

» Sea salt and freshly ground black pepper

» 1 tsp dried thyme

» Pinch of ground cloves

» 4 lb/1.8 kg hanger steak

» 2 tbsp vegetable oil

» 2 yellow onions, finely chopped

» 4 carrots, peeled and finely chopped

» 2 celery stalks, peeled and finely chopped

» 1 cup/240 ml dry red wine

» 2 cups/480 ml water

» 1 tbsp tomato paste

» 4 tbsp/55 g unsalted butter

Preheat the oven to 200°F/95°C.

Stir the flour, 1 tsp salt, ½ tsp pepper, thyme, and cloves together on a sheet of aluminum foil. Dredge the steaks in the flour mixture, and set aside any remaining flour mixture.

In a large Dutch oven over high heat, heat 1 tbsp of the oil. When the oil is hot, add the steaks and sear to brown nicely on both sides, about 5 minutes per side. Transfer the steaks to a plate.

Reduce the heat to medium, add the remaining 1 tbsp oil to the pot, and sauté the onions, carrots, and celery until lightly browned, about 8 minutes. Add the remaining flour mixture and stir to coat everything with the flour. Cook until the flour browns lightly, about 4 minutes. Add the wine and bring to a boil, stirring constantly. Add the water and tomato paste, and stir while the liquid comes to a boil. Return the steaks to the pan along with any juices that have accumulated on the plate. Cover and bake until the meat is fork-tender and liquid in the pan is lightly thickened, about 6 hours.

Uncover the pot and raise the oven temperature to 425°F/220°C/gas 7. Cook for 15 more minutes to brown the surface of the meat.

Transfer the steaks to a cutting board and let rest for 10 minutes. Strain the sauce through a fine-mesh sieve into a bowl; discard the solids. Return the sauce to the pot and bring to a boil, cooking to reduce and thicken to the desired consistency. Remove from the heat and swirl in the butter. Taste and adjust the seasoning. Carve the steaks as desired, ladle the sauce over, and serve.

MEATLOAF

The secret to great meatloaf is in the filler. The special flavor of excellent-quality meat, including free-range, grass-fed, and organic products, will shine in this rustic loaf, and meat certainly makes it hearty and nutritious . . . but it is the modest pantry staples like bread crumbs, milk, egg, onion, ketchup, mustard, and Worcestershire sauce that make a luscious and savory meatloaf to be loved. Add to that list one more ingredient—time. By lowering the heat and extending the baking time, you alter the cooking science behind this comfort-food favorite. No part of the loaf gets crispy or tough or dry, and everything melds into a silky-smooth, tender chewiness. This meatloaf is intentionally huge to ensure lots of leftovers for sandwiches.

PREP TIME: 10 minutes	**COOKING TIME:** 6 to 8 hours	**STORE:** for up to 4 days, covered in the refrigerator. Reheat gently in a low oven, or serve cold (see Getting Creative box, facing page).	*Makes* **8** *servings, with leftovers*

» 2 cups/110 g fresh bread crumbs

» ¾ cup/180 ml milk

» 1 medium yellow onion, coarsely shredded

» 2 large eggs

» ¾ cup/180 ml ketchup

» 2 tbsp Worcestershire sauce

» 1 tbsp brown mustard

» 1 tsp fine sea salt

» ½ tsp freshly ground black pepper

» 1½ lb/680 g ground beef

» ¾ lb/340 g ground veal

» ¾ lb/340 g ground pork

Preheat the oven to 200°F/95°C.

In a large bowl, combine the bread crumbs and milk and stir until uniformly moistened. Add the onion, eggs, ketchup, Worcestershire, mustard, salt, and pepper and mix to combine thoroughly. Add the meat and mix gently with your hands just until everything is combined; do not overmix. Pack into a large (at least 2-qt/2-l) loaf pan. Cover with aluminum foil and bake until an instant-read thermometer inserted into the center registers 190°F/88°C or higher, 6 to 8 hours.

Remove from the oven and let the meatloaf rest for 10 minutes. Drain any liquid that has accumulated in the pan. Turn the meatloaf out onto a platter. Cut into slices and serve.

VARIATION: IN A SLOW COOKER

Instead of packing the meat mixture into a loaf pan, drape a double-thick strip of heavy-duty aluminum foil about 6 in/15 cm wide across the bottom and up the sides of a 5- to 6-qt/4.5- to 5.7-l, oval-shaped slow cooker, and form the meat into an oval loaf on the foil. Cover and cook on low for 6 to 8 hours.

GETTING CREATIVE

Similar to country paté, meatloaf is delicious served cold. To make it more paté-worthy, gussy up your meatloaf with other ingredients like toasted nuts, blanched vegetables (asparagus, carrots, green beans), diced ham, or leftover roasted meat, layering them with the meatloaf mixture in the loaf pan. Bake as directed, then let cool and refrigerate until well chilled. Serve cold with a selection of mustard and pickles.

SAUSAGE-STUFFED
PORK CHOPS
WITH CREAM GRAVY

Modern pork is given an internal-doneness temperature of 154°F/66°C—a happy dip from the 180°F/82°C standard recommended when pork was cooked to be salmonella-safe rather than delicious. However, at about the same time that salmonella disappeared, pork was beginning to be reengineered for less fat. The amount of internal fat in the animal accordingly plummeted, but the lean meat often tastes dry and grainy when overcooked by even a few degrees. All of which makes pork a prime candidate for slow baking. There's one hitch: most oven thermostats don't register below 175°F/80°C, which is about 15°F/8°C higher than you want the interior of your pork to be. The solution: in this recipe, the pork is protected by a moist, fat-laced stuffing, so the heat moves through the chop more slowly. A cloak of creamy sauce for serving makes sure every bite is juicy perfection.

PREP TIME: 30 minutes	**COOKING TIME:** about 2½ hours	**STORE:** Best served immediately.	*Makes* **4** *servings*

FOR THE SAUSAGE STUFFING:

» 2 tbsp unsalted butter

» ½ medium yellow onion, finely chopped

» 1 small apple, peeled, cored, and finely chopped

» ½ tsp sea salt

» ¼ tsp freshly ground black pepper

» 5 oz/140 g mild Italian sausage

» 1 tsp chopped fresh rosemary

» 1 tbsp chopped fresh flat-leaf parsley

» ¼ cup/30 g dried bread crumbs

» ¼ cup/60 ml Old Chicken Broth (page 91)

» 4 thick bone-in pork rib chops, about 12 oz/340 g each

» 1 strip thick-cut bacon

» 2 tbsp all-purpose flour

» 1 cup/240 ml milk

» 1 cup/240 ml Old Chicken Broth (page 91)

To make the stuffing: Melt the butter in a large cast-iron skillet over medium heat. Add the onion and apple and sauté just until tender, about 5 minutes. Season with the salt and pepper. Add the sausage, rosemary, and parsley and sauté until the sausage loses its raw look, about 3 minutes. Add the bread crumbs and broth and stir until everything is combined. Remove from the heat and let cool.

Meanwhile, preheat the oven to 175°F/80°C. Cut a pocket in the meaty side of each pork chop and pack each with one-fourth of the stuffing. Secure the opening with a toothpick.

Wipe the skillet clean with a damp cloth and put it over medium heat. Cook the bacon until crisp, about 5 minutes. Discard the bacon, or (and who wouldn't?) transfer to paper towels to drain and have a snack.

Raise the heat under the skillet to high. When the fat is hot, add the pork chops and brown on both sides, about 2 minutes per side. Remove from the heat and cover the pan.

Bake until the chops register at least 160°F/71°C on an instant-read thermometer, about 2 hours.

When the chops are done, transfer to a platter. Using a heavy pot holder, put the skillet over medium heat. Add the flour to the skillet and cook in the pan juices, stirring, until the mixture turns a light beige color. Stir in the milk and broth, bring to a simmer, and cook, stirring often, until a lightly thickened gravy forms, about 5 minutes. Pour the gravy over the chops and serve.

SLOW-BAKED

CHOUCROUTE

Choucroute, served at every beer hall in France east of Lorraine, is the hot dog and sauerkraut dish of Alsace. Because cooking choucroute is more a matter of marrying flavors than cooking ingredients to doneness, your timing can extend or shrink to fit your schedule. But remember, the longer the choucroute simmers in the low heat, the deeper the flavors will get—and this easy-to-assemble dish yields an instant dinner picnic without any work from you after it goes in the oven. Feel free to vary the sausages according to what's available. Serve with brown mustard, a nice rye bread, and cold beer or white wine.

| **PREP TIME:** 15 minutes | **COOKING TIME:** 4½ to 8½ hours | **STORE:** for up to 3 days, covered in the refrigerator. Reheat gently in a low oven. | *Makes* **8** *servings* |

» 4 bacon strips

» 3 lb/1.4 kg sauerkraut, drained

» 12 small red-skinned potatoes, scrubbed and halved

» 1 large yellow onion, thinly sliced

» 2 bay leaves

» 8 juniper berries

» ⅛ tsp ground cloves

» 1 tsp ground coriander

» 3 garlic cloves, coarsely chopped

» Freshly ground black pepper

» 1 lb/455 g boneless smoked pork butt, cut into 8 slices

» 4 knockwurst, quartered

» 4 bratwurst, quartered

» One 12-oz/360-ml bottle lager beer

Preheat the oven to 200°F/95°C.

In a large Dutch oven, cook the bacon over medium heat until the fat is rendered and the bacon is almost completely crisp, about 10 minutes. Transfer the bacon to paper towels to drain, then crumble. Put the sauerkraut in a bowl, add the crumbled bacon, and toss to mix.

Return the pot with the bacon fat to medium heat. Add the potatoes and cook, stirring often, until lightly browned, about 15 minutes. Add the onion and cook until translucent, about 5 minutes. Remove from the heat.

Add half of the sauerkraut to the pot and spread in an even layer. Scatter half of all the spices and the garlic over the top, and arrange the pork slices and sausages on top. Cover with the remaining sauerkraut and spices. Pour the beer over all. Cover and bake for 4 to 8 hours.

Serve hot or warm.

VARIATION: IN A SLOW COOKER

Following the recipe, cook the bacon in a large skillet, then cook the potatoes and onion in the fat. Layer everything in a 6-qt/5.7-l slow cooker and cook on low for 6 to 8 hours.

 BBQ RIBS

If you don't have the gear for famed "low and slow" barbecuing—such as a grill with an external fire box or a full-on barbecue pit—this method of slow-cooking spareribs is as close as you will get to the real thing. Setting an oven to the doneness temperature of pork ribs makes them virtually "warm" their way to doneness. The succulent rib meat does not dry out; the flavors have hours to penetrate; and all you have to do is walk away. Although the ribs will be done in 6 hours, you can let them cook longer; these babies cannot overcook.

PREP TIME: 3 minutes	**COOKING TIME:** about 6 hours	**STORE:** for up to 3 days, covered in the refrigerator. Reheat gently in a low oven.	*Makes* **4** *servings*

» 1 cup/240 ml Dark Beer BBQ Sauce (facing page) or your favorite store-bought or homemade barbecue sauce

» 2 lb/910 g pork spareribs, cut into individual ribs

Preheat the oven to 200°F/95°C.

Pour half of the sauce into a 9-by-13-by-2-in/23-by-33-by-5-cm baking dish. Roll the ribs in the sauce to coat and pour the rest of the sauce over the top. Cover the dish with aluminum foil and bake until the rib meat is very tender and almost falling off the bone, about 6 hours.

Raise the oven temperature to 450°F/230°C/gas 8. Remove the foil and bake until the ribs are browned, about 15 minutes longer. Serve immediately.

VARIATION: IN A SLOW COOKER
Follow the recipe using the crock of a 6-qt/5.7-l slow cooker in place of the baking dish and cook on low for about 6 hours. Brown the ribs for a few minutes under the broiler when they are finished.

Dark Beer BBQ Sauce

This super-rich, lacquer-like barbecue sauce makes everything taste meatier. Maybe it's the dark roasted flavors of the molasses or the subtle yeasty umami from the dark beer. Whatever the cause, it is a great flavor enhancer for pork, beef, chicken, or "meaty" vegetables, like eggplant or portabella mushrooms. Store for up to 1 week in an airtight container in the refrigerator.

Makes about 2 cups

» 2 cups/480 ml rich, dark beer such as porter or stout
» 1 cup/240 ml ketchup
» ¼ cup/60 ml spicy brown mustard
» ⅓ cup/75 ml molasses
» 2 tsp sea salt
» 2 tsp freshly ground black pepper
» 2 tbsp hot-pepper sauce

In a saucepan over medium-high heat, bring the beer to a boil. Simmer briskly until reduced by half, about 10 minutes. Add the ketchup, mustard, molasses, salt, and pepper and stir to mix well. Simmer, stirring often, until thickened, about 5 minutes. Remove from the heat and let cool. Stir in the hot-pepper sauce.

LAMB SHANKS
∼ SLOW-BAKED ∼
WITH ZA'ATAR AND OVEN-DRIED TOMATOES

Lamb shanks ain't dainty. Because they are smaller than the shanks of veal or pork, they are not cut into designer cross sections for serving. Lamb shanks are served whole; the meat caramelizes to a beautiful rich brown around (and almost falling off of) the bone, with each shank presenting pretty much a perfect portion. These shanks are rubbed with a classic Middle Eastern *za'atar*—a spice blend of sesame, thyme, and sumac leaves—and infused, during a long, slow cooking nestled in a rich mix full of flavor-packed, chewy oven-dried tomatoes, with the very essence of tomato.

It's easy to make your own *za'atar* with the recipe here, and the sumac you need to buy will likely inspire you to try other Middle Eastern recipes. You can buy prepared *za'atar* at gourmet and online shops. It's also super-easy to make the Oven-Dried Tomatoes—but note, you'll want to make them the day before; they need 6 hours in and of themselves.

PREP TIME: 20 minutes (including making the *za'atar*)	**COOKING TIME:** 4½ to 8½ hours	**STORE:** for up to 4 days, covered in the refrigerator. Reheat gently in a low oven.	*Makes* **4** *servings*

» 2 tbsp *za'atar* (recipe follows)

» 2 tsp coarse sea salt

» 4 lamb shanks, about 1 lb/455 g each

» 3 tbsp olive oil

» 2 large yellow onions, coarsely shredded

» 4 garlic cloves, minced

» 2 tbsp all-purpose flour

» 1 cup/240 ml full-bodied red wine such as Merlot or Cabernet

» 1 cup/240 ml good-quality low-sodium beef broth

» ½ recipe Oven-Dried Tomatoes (page 50)

In a small bowl, stir together the *za'atar* and salt. Rub half of the spice mixture over the lamb shanks and set aside for about 30 minutes.

Preheat the oven to 200°F/95°C.

In a large Dutch oven, heat 1½ tbsp of the olive oil over medium-high heat. When the oil is hot, add the lamb shanks and cook, turning as needed, until nicely browned on all sides, about 10 minutes total. Transfer to a plate.

Add the remaining 1½ tbsp olive oil to the pot, reduce the heat to medium, and add the onions. Sauté the onions until lightly browned, about 5 minutes. Add the garlic and flour and continue cooking, stirring constantly, until everything is well browned, about 3 minutes more. Add the wine and bring to a boil, again stirring constantly. Stir in the broth and remaining spice mix and return to a boil. Cook, stirring, until the sauce thickens slightly, about 4 minutes.

Return the shanks to the pot along with any juices that accumulated on the plate. Add the tomatoes, cover, and bake for 6 to 8 hours.

Using tongs, transfer the shanks to a serving platter. Skim the fat from the cooking liquid. Spoon the sauce over the shanks and serve.

VARIATION: IN A SLOW COOKER

Season and brown the shanks and make the sauce in the Dutch oven as directed in the recipe. Transfer to a 6-qt/5.7-l slow cooker. Pour the sauce over the shanks and top with the tomatoes. Cook for 4 to 5 hours on high, 6 to 8 hours on low.

Za'atar

Sumac is available at many spice markets or online at www.penzeys.com. Store *za'atar* for up to 1 month in a cool, dark place in an airtight container.

Makes about ½ cup

» ⅓ cup/15 g dried thyme
» 2 tbsp dried sumac
» 1 tbsp sesame seeds, toasted (see Toasting Sesame Seeds or Pine Nuts box, page 39)
» 1 tsp sea salt

Combine all of the ingredients in a mortar and pound with a pestle until coarsely ground and evenly mixed. Alternatively, use a mini food processor or spice grinder, but be careful to pulse the processor in brief spurts so you don't turn the thyme into powder.

DUCK RAGÙ
WITH CHERRIES

Ragùs are much-loved long-simmered meat sauces, brimming with tradition. In the old days, the sauce pot sputtered lazily on the back of a wood-burning stove, and in the present, the wisps of fragrant steam drifting through the kitchen continue to be a timeless pleasure. Long cooking on the stove top, however, risks scorching and requires spurts of attentive stirring. I find that the easiest way to achieve the perfect slow simmer is in the surrounding heat of a low oven.

Since the advent of jarred meat sauce, most Americans think of meat sauce as a tomato sauce flavored with browned ground meat. Don't let the manufacturers fool you; real meat sauce is loaded with meat, about 90 percent by weight. The fatty, flavor-packed duck in this sauce makes it especially rich. Slow cooking tenderizes the meat, and long cooking practically liquefies the protein into an ideal, rib-sticking thickness. If the sauce gets *too* thick, it can be loosened with a little pasta water just before serving.

CHILLING TIME: 40 minutes **PREP TIME:** 30 minutes	**COOKING TIME:** about 7 hours	**STORE:** for up to 3 days, covered in the refrigerator. Reheat gently in a low oven.	*Makes* **6** *servings*

» 2 lb/910 g boneless, skinless duck breast, cut into 1-in/2.5-cm chunks

» 4 oz/115 g bacon, cut into ½-in/12-mm pieces

» ½ tsp fine sea salt

» ¼ tsp freshly ground pepper

» 1 medium yellow onion, minced

» 1 medium carrot, peeled and minced

» 1 celery stalk, minced

» 1 garlic clove, minced

» 8 canned plum tomatoes, crushed

» 1 cup/240 ml dry red wine

» 1 fresh rosemary sprig

» 3 fresh thyme sprigs

» One 2-oz/55-g piece Parmesan cheese rind

» 8 oz/225 g fresh or canned sour cherries, pitted and quartered

» 1 lb/455 g wide flat pasta such as fettuccine or farfalle

Spread the duck meat and bacon in a single layer on a baking sheet or other shallow pan that will fit into your freezer and freeze until firm but not solid, about 40 minutes. Working in small batches in a food processor, pulse the meat and fat until finely chopped. Stir in the salt and pepper.

Preheat the oven to 250°F/120°C/gas ½.

Heat a large Dutch oven or large deep skillet over medium heat. Add the ground meat and cook until it is no longer red, stirring and scraping the bottom of the pan to cook the meat evenly, about 10 minutes.

Add the onion, carrot, and celery and cook until the vegetables are barely tender, about 5 minutes. Add the garlic and tomatoes and cook until aromatic, about 5 minutes. Raise the heat to medium-high and add the wine. Simmer until the aroma of alcohol diminishes, about 1 minute.

Add 1 qt/960 ml water along with the rosemary and thyme sprigs and the Parmesan rind. Cover and bake until the duck is falling-apart tender, the sauce thickens, and the flavors are rich

- » **4 tbsp/55 g unsalted butter, cut into small cubes**
- » **⅓ cup/45 g finely grated Parmesan cheese, preferably Parmigiano-Reggiano**
- » **Small handful of chopped fresh flat-leaf parsley**

and blended, about 6 hours. (The sauce can be made up to this point up to 4 days in advance. Cover and refrigerate until ready to continue.)

Add the cherries and cook until soft, about 30 minutes if using fresh, 10 minutes if using canned. Meanwhile, cook the pasta (see Cooking and Saucing Pasta box, below).

Remove the Parmesan rind and herb sprigs. Swirl the butter into the hot sauce just before tossing it with the pasta. Garnish with the grated Parmesan and the parsley and serve immediately.

VARIATION: IN A SLOW COOKER
Follow the recipe through adding the wine and bring the mixture to a boil, then transfer the ragù to a 6-qt/5.7-l slow cooker. Add only 2 cups water along with the herbs and Parmesan rind and cook on low for 4 to 6 hours. Add the cherries during the last hour.

COOKING AND SAUCING PASTA

Bring a large pot of salted water to a boil. Italian tradition tells us to salt pasta water to the taste of the sea, which is 3.5 percent salt, so don't hold back on the salt—to bring 1 gal/3.8 l of fresh water to the saltiness of the sea takes about 2 cupped handfuls of coarse salt, preferably sea salt. Add fresh or dried pasta to the rapidly boiling water and cook until the pasta is tender but firm, about 4 minutes for fresh pasta or 9 minutes for dried (or according to the package directions). Before draining, ladle a couple cups of the cooking water into a small pitcher and reserve. The starch from the pasta gives the water a creamy consistency that is great for adjusting a thick pasta sauce without watering it down.

CHAPTER 3

· SLOW ·

SIMMERING

Liquid is extremely effective at transferring heat—much better than air. Here is a cooking parable: You are baking a potato in a 400°F/200°C/gas 6 oven. You want to check to see whether the spud is done so you open the oven and give it a squeeze. "Not yet," you decide. You remove your hand and close the oven door. You are also boiling another potato in a large pot of water. The temperature of the water is 212°F/100°C, half the temperature of the aforementioned oven. You want to see if the potato is done so you stick your hand in the water to give it a squeeze. Ouch!! Lesson learned: liquid *is* more effective at transferring heat than is air.

This means slow simmering is a more effective way of cooking than almost any other method, but it also means that ingredients are more likely to overcook when liquid is present. It is important then to know the temperature of the hot liquid you are cooking in. You could of course use a thermometer to monitor the cooking temp, but because it is difficult to maintain a constant temperature in a pot of water on a stove top, constantly checking it with a thermometer is cumbersome. Given that thermometers are notoriously inaccurate as well, it's beneficial to learn the nuances of visual signs of heating water.

At sea level, water at a rolling boil is 212°F/100°C. When there are just bubbles at the edge of the pot the temperature is 190°F/88°C. And when the surface of the water is shivering it is at about 175°F/80°C.

Boiling occurs because water at the bottom of a heating pot is hotter than the water at the top. When the water at the bottom gets hot enough to turn into steam, the steam bubbles rise up to the surface and burst: the water boils. Because the temperature of the boiling point of water is determined by how much heat it takes to make a steam bubble burst through the surface of the water, the air pressure on the surface of the liquid affects the temperature. As the air pressure increases, the temperature of boiling water gets hotter. This is the premise behind pressure cooking. And when there is less air weighing down the water's surface, the boiling point decreases. The higher the elevation at which you are boiling, the less atmosphere there is to weigh down the water. So for every 1000 ft/305 m of elevation above sea level, the temperature of boiling/simmering water drops by 2°F/1°C.

ROOT VEGETABLE

BORSCHT

Many vegetables are actually fruits—bell peppers, tomatoes, cucumbers, eggplant—and fruits don't last. They are soft and wet and prone to decay, and therefore have to be used soon after harvesting. But other veggies can hold it together—those that are fibrous and firm, offering edible roots, stems, and meaty leaves. These can be stored for months, long into the winter, and so we call them winter vegetables. Where fruit-veggies are soft and juicy enough to eat raw or with minimal cooking, winter vegetables need simmering time; for most of them the longer and slower, the better.

Borscht, the Ukrainian root-and-cabbage soup, perks on the back of the stove all day long. Because everything in it is impervious to breakdown, there's no chance of overcooking. Most of the borscht eaten in the States is summer borscht, which is made entirely from beets and onions, and is served cold. Winter borscht usually contains meat. I have kept this one vegetarian, although adding a soup bone along with the cabbage is certain to please meat eaters.

PREP TIME: 20 minutes	COOKING TIME: about 6½ hours	STORE: for up to 1 week, covered in the refrigerator. Reheat gently over low heat or in a low oven.	*Makes* **6** TO **8** *servings*

- » 1 tbsp canola oil
- » 2 large yellow onions, cut into ½-in/12-mm dice
- » 2 medium carrots, peeled and cut into ½-in/12-mm dice
- » 1 medium parsnip, peeled and cut into ½-in/12-mm dice
- » 1 medium turnip, peeled and cut into ½-in/12-mm dice
- » 3 medium beets, peeled and cut into ½-in/12-mm dice
- » About ¼ head green cabbage (about ½ lb/225 g), cut into ½-in/12-mm dice
- » 1 cup/240 ml full-bodied dry red wine such as Cabernet or Merlot
- » 2 tsp dried thyme
- » 1 tsp dried rosemary
- » Pinch of ground cloves
- » 1 bay leaf
- » 8 fresh dill sprigs, chopped
- » One 28-oz/800-g can diced tomatoes, with juice
- » 1 to 2 tbsp red wine vinegar
- » About ½ cup/120 ml sour cream (optional)

In a large Dutch oven over medium heat, heat the oil. Add the onions, carrots, parsnip, and turnip and stir to coat with the oil. Cover and cook, stirring occasionally but keeping the pot covered as much as possible, until the vegetables are tender and aromatic, about 10 minutes.

Add the beets and the cabbage and toss to combine. Add the wine and boil for 3 minutes.

Add 6 cups/1.4 l water, the thyme, rosemary, cloves, bay leaf, and dill and stir to mix well. Stir in the tomatoes with their juices and the vinegar and bring to a simmer. Reduce the heat to maintain a very gentle simmer, cover, and cook until the soup is deep burgundy red and all of the vegetables are very tender, about 6 hours.

Purée the soup with an immersion blender directly in the cooking pot, or in batches in a standing blender. Serve hot with dollops of sour cream.

VARIATION: IN A SLOW COOKER

Follow the recipe directions, heating to a simmer in a Dutch oven or in a large, deep skillet. Pour into a 6-qt/5.7-l slow cooker and cook on low for 6 hours or on high for 3 hours. Finish as directed.

MOLTEN
❧ CAULIFLOWER ❧

Cauliflower is a powerhouse of pectin, the fibrous "glue" in the cell walls of many plants. During slow cooking, this quality of cauliflower is easily coaxed to produce exceedingly tender renditions for sides and even sauces. This recipe yields both; some of the cauliflower is concentrated and caramelized in the oven, and some is simmered into a creamy sauce. The two elements put this lush vegetarian casserole in stereo for cauliflower lovers, and make it completely satisfying. It was inspired by *Cauliflower in a Cast-Iron Pot,* made deliciously popular by Jeremy Fox, the original chef at Ubuntu, a visionary vegetarian restaurant in Napa, California. This casserole only needs to cook for an hour, but it can go another hour with no harm, like most slow-cooked treasures.

PREP TIME: 15 minutes	COOKING TIME: 2 to 3 hours	STORE: for up to 3 days, covered in the refrigerator. Reheat gently in a low oven.	*Makes* **4** *servings*

» 2 heads cauliflower, trimmed and cored, broken into florets and florets thinly sliced

» 4 tbsp olive oil

» 6 tbsp/85 g unsalted butter

» 1 medium yellow onion, finely chopped

» 4 garlic cloves, finely chopped

» 1 tbsp good-quality curry powder or Homemade Curry Seasoning (recipe follows)

» 1 cup/240 ml milk

» Sea salt and freshly ground black pepper

» 4 slices day-old bread

» 1 tsp chopped fresh flat-leaf parsley

Preheat the oven to 350°F/180°C/gas 4.

Put about two-thirds of the cauliflower on a rimmed baking sheet. Drizzle with 2 tbsp of the olive oil and toss to coat. Roast until tender and browned on the edges, about 40 minutes.

Meanwhile, in a small skillet, melt the butter over medium heat and cook until it starts to brown. Remove from the heat, pour into a small bowl, and set aside. Heat the remaining 2 tbsp olive oil in a saucepan over medium heat. Add the onion and cook slowly until very tender and lightly browned, about 20 minutes. Add the garlic and curry and cook until very aromatic, about 5 minutes longer.

Spoon 2 tbsp of the onion mixture into the bowl with the melted butter. Stir to mix well and set aside again. Add the remaining one-third cauliflower to the saucepan with the onion, along with the milk and just enough water so the cauliflower is barely covered with liquid. Bring to a simmer and cook until the cauliflower is very tender, about 20 minutes. Season with salt and pepper. Transfer to a blender and process to a smooth purée, or use an immersion blender and purée in the pan. Strain through a fine-mesh sieve if needed; you want a silky sauce.

When the roasted cauliflower is done, remove from the oven and set aside. Brush the bread with the seasoned melted butter and toast in the oven for about 5 minutes. Remove from the oven, let cool slightly, and cut into ¼-in/6-mm croutons.

Reduce the oven temperature to 250°F/120°C/gas ½. In a 6-cup/1.4-l casserole, make layers of croutons, roasted cauliflower, and sauce, starting and ending with a sparse layer of croutons. Cover and bake until the mixture is bubbly, 1 to 2 hours. Let cool slightly, sprinkle with parsley, and scoop to serve.

Homemade Curry Seasoning

Curries are complicated blends of dozens of spices, and there are hundreds of traditional combinations. The following is a reliable Madras-style curry. It can be made many times more fragrant if you take the trouble to toast and grind some of the spices. Whole cumin and mustard seed can be toasted quickly by heating a cast-iron skillet over high heat for about 5 minutes. Remove the pan from the heat and swirl the spices in the hot pan until they are aromatic, about 1 minute. Grind in a spice grinder or clean coffee mill.

Makes ¼ cup

» **2 tsp ground coriander**
» **2 tsp powdered ginger**
» **2 tsp ground turmeric**
» **1½ tsp ground cumin seed**
» **1 tsp ground mustard**
» **1 tsp minced dried garlic**
» **½ tsp cinnamon**
» **¼ tsp ground cardamom**
» **¼ tsp crushed red pepper flakes**
» **1 tsp fine sea salt**
» **½ tsp freshly ground black pepper**

Mix together the coriander, ginger, turmeric, cumin seed, mustard, garlic, cinnamon, cardamom, red pepper flakes, salt, and black pepper. Store up to 1 month in a closed container in a dark cabinet.

COUSCOUS
OF WINTER SQUASH AND TUBERS

This vegan stew of hearty squash, sweet potatoes, and other roots is redolent with the seasoning of North Africa: saffron, turmeric, coriander, cumin, and cinnamon. Couscous, those tiny orbs of pasta now loved the world over, is traditionally a slower cooking product, still steamed in its homelands and by purists in a perforated vessel (a couscoussier) set above boiling water or a simmering stew; but now this type of raw couscous is rare. Instant couscous is far more readily available, and much easier to use.

PREP TIME: 25 minutes	COOKING TIME: 2½ hours	STORE: for up to 3 days, covered in the refrigerator. Reheat gently in a low oven.	*Makes* **10** *servings*

» 3 large yellow onions

» 3 carrots, peeled

» 3 celery stalks

» 1 head garlic

» 1 small butternut squash

» 1 medium acorn squash

» 2 white turnips

» 1 large sweet potato

» 2 small zucchini

» 1 lb/455 g plum tomatoes

» 6 tbsp/85 g unsalted butter, cut into chunks

» 1 tbsp ground coriander

» 2 tsp ground cumin seed

» 1 tsp saffron

» 1 tsp ground turmeric

» 1 cinnamon stick, broken in half

» 1 dried chile pepper such as cayenne

» 2 qt/2 l good-quality low-sodium vegetable broth

» Sea salt and freshly ground black pepper

» 1 tsp olive oil

» 2 cups/370 g instant whole-wheat couscous

» ½ cup/120 ml Harissa (page 86; optional)

Coarsely chop the onions. Cut the carrots into 1-in/2.5-cm chunks. Trim the celery and cut into 1-in/2.5-cm chunks. Break the head of garlic into cloves and peel them. Peel, seed, and chop both squashes into 1-in/2.5-cm chunks. Peel the turnips and slice them into thick rounds. Peel the sweet potato and slice it into thick rounds. Slice the zucchini crosswise into 1-in/2.5-cm chunks. Quarter the tomatoes.

Melt the butter in a large Dutch oven over medium heat. Add the onions, carrots, celery, and garlic and sauté until the onions are translucent, about 6 minutes. Add the coriander, cumin, saffron, turmeric, cinnamon, chile, and broth. Bring to a simmer. Season with salt and pepper.

Add the squashes, turnips, and sweet potato. Reduce the heat to low, cover, and simmer very gently for 1 hour. Add the zucchini and tomatoes and simmer until everything is very tender, about 1 hour longer. Discard the cinnamon stick.

About 5 minutes before the stew is done, bring 2 cups/480 ml water to a boil. Stir in the olive oil and season with salt and pepper. Stir in the couscous and remove from the heat. Cover and let the couscous steep for 5 minutes.

Fluff the couscous with a fork and toss with a little of the Harissa, if desired. Mound on a wide platter. Make a deep well in the center of the couscous and fill with the vegetables and broth. Pour some of the cooking liquid over all to moisten. Serve with additional cooking liquid and more Harissa on the side.

Harissa

Harissa is a commonplace North African condiment composed of chiles and aromatic spices, such as coriander, ground and made into a sauce with hot water and oil. It is typically stirred into ground meat dishes, as with merguez sausage, and is often used as a topping for roasted meats and fish. But harissa is perhaps most closely identified as a relish for couscous. Good-quality harissa is readily available in Middle Eastern groceries and many supermarkets, but it is very easy, and much better, to make your own.

Makes ½ cup/95 g

» **1 dried ancho or guajillo chile, stemmed and seeded**
» **1 dried cayenne or piri piri chile, stemmed and seeded**
» **⅓ cup/75 ml hot water**
» **½ tsp ground coriander**
» **½ tsp sea salt**
» **½ tsp ground cumin**
» **1 tsp hot paprika**
» **Olive oil as needed**

Put the chiles in a heatproof bowl and pour the hot water over. Let soak for 30 minutes. Drain.

Combine the chiles, coriander, salt, cumin, and paprika in a mortar and pound with a pestle until finely ground. Add a little olive oil and pound to work into a paste. Continue adding oil to make a liquid. (Alternatively, make the sauce in a mini food processor.) Use as a seasoning with couscous. Store, covered in refrigerator, for up to 3 months.

CHICKEN WINGS

Slow-baking chicken wings in a spicy soy glaze imbues the meat with pungent flavors and aromas and burnishes the skin like mahogany. Because the wings are so slowly baked, there is little need for added fat, and the flavor is intense. Crank the oven up high for the last 10 minutes to crisp the skin and thicken the glaze.

CHILLING TIME: 12 to 24 hours	COOKING TIME: about	STORE: for up to 3 days, covered	*Makes*
PREP TIME: 5 minutes	3 hours	in the refrigerator. Rewarm gently in a low oven or over low heat.	**4** *servings*

» 4 lb/1.8 kg chicken wings, cut into sections at the joints, tapered wing tips trimmed and discarded

» Coarse sea salt and freshly ground black pepper

» ⅔ cup/165 ml soy sauce

» ⅔ cup/130 g firmly packed dark brown sugar

» 1 tsp dark sesame oil

» ¼ tsp cayenne pepper

» ⅛ tsp hot chili powder, preferably habanero

» 2 garlic cloves, minced

Combine the chicken wing pieces with a generous amount of salt and pepper in a large zippered plastic bag. Close the bag tightly and refrigerate for at least 12 hours or up to 24 hours.

Preheat the oven to 225°F/110°C/gas ¼. Transfer the chicken to a baking dish in a single layer without crowding.

In a small saucepan, stir together the soy sauce, brown sugar, sesame oil, cayenne, chili powder, and garlic and heat to a simmer, stirring to dissolve the sugar. Pour over the chicken. Cover the baking dish with aluminum foil and cook until the chicken is nearly falling off the bone, about 3 hours.

Raise the oven temperature to 450°F/230°C/gas 8 and continue baking until the chicken browns and the sauce thickens into a glaze, about 10 minutes longer. Watch carefully near the end of the cooking time to avoid burning. Toss the wings in the sauce to coat and serve.

VARIATION: IN A SLOW COOKER
Follow the recipe, cooking the chicken in a 6-qt/5.7-l slow cooker on high for 3 to 4 hours, instead of a baking dish in the oven. When the wings are cooked through, transfer to a bowl. Simmer the sauce with the lid of the cooker off until it thickens, about 10 minutes longer. Toss the wings in the thickened sauce and serve.

CHICKEN

CACCIATORE

Cacciatore **means "hunter's style"** in Italian cuisine, and though it means "tomato sauce" to most Americans, traditionally tomato was a garnish rather than the main attraction. Classic cacciatore is made from the ingredients a hunter would find as he treks through woods and fields: mushrooms, forest herbs, wild onions. This recipe is similar to one that I developed for my slow cooker book, *Art of the Slow Cooker*, but with one huge difference—it is simmered in an oven. Because slow cookers trap moisture, they turn out chicken that tastes steamed rather than braised, and slow cooker sauces can be watery. You can fix the sauce issue by cutting the amount of liquid in the recipe by half (see variation), but the steamed-meat texture can be changed only by moving the cooking process to a cooker that allows for some evaporation, like an oven. In addition, you can set an oven's temperature lower than a slow cooker for chicken meat that falls off the bone without overcooking.

As with all slow-simmered meats, lowering the cooking temperature of cacciatore yields exceptionally tender meat and a beautifully nuanced sauce.

PREP TIME: 15 minutes	COOKING TIME: about 6½ hours	STORE: for up to 3 days, covered in the refrigerator. Rewarm gently in a low oven or over low heat.	*Makes* **4** *servings*

» ⅓ cup/40 g all-purpose flour

» Fine sea salt and freshly ground black pepper

» 1 tbsp Homemade Italian Seasoning (page 90)

» 4 lb/1.8 kg bone-in, skinless chicken pieces such as legs, thighs, and breast halves (see Poultry Skin box, page 179)

» 2 to 3 tbsp olive oil

» 1 yellow onion, chopped

» 8 oz/225 g white mushrooms, brushed clean and sliced

» 2 garlic cloves, minced

» 1 cup/240 ml dry white wine

» 1 cup/240 ml Old Chicken Broth (page 91)

» One 15-oz/430-g can diced tomatoes, with juice

» 1 tbsp anchovy paste or finely chopped anchovy fillets

» 3 tbsp chopped fresh flat-leaf parsley

Preheat the oven to 200°F/95°C.

Mix together the flour, 1 tsp salt, ½ tsp pepper, and Italian seasoning on a sheet of aluminum foil. Toss the chicken pieces in the seasoned flour to coat completely.

In a large Dutch oven, pour enough olive oil to coat the bottom generously and place over medium-high heat. Heat until the oil is shimmering hot. Working in batches as needed to avoid crowding the pot, add the chicken pieces to the hot oil and cook until browned nicely on all sides, about 10 minutes per batch. Transfer the chicken pieces to a plate as they are finished. When all of the chicken is browned, set aside. Do not discard the remaining flour mixture.

If the pot seems dry, add more oil. Add the onion and mushrooms and sauté until the vegetables soften, about 5 minutes. Add the garlic and sauté until aromatic, about 30 seconds more.

Add the reserved flour mixture and stir until dissolved into the oil in the pan. Cook, stirring constantly, until the flour is lightly browned, about 2 minutes. Add the wine and bring to a boil. Add the broth, tomatoes with their juices, and anchovy paste and stir to mix well. Return to a simmer. Taste and adjust the seasoning with salt and pepper, if needed. Return the chicken to the pot along with any juices that accumulated on the plate. Cover the pot, transfer to the oven, and cook until all of the flavors are blended and the chicken meat is falling-off-the-bone tender, about 6 hours. Garnish with the parsley and serve.

VARIATION: IN A SLOW COOKER

Follow the recipe, but cut the amount of wine and broth in half. Cook in a 6-qt/5.7-l slow cooker on low for 5 to 7 hours.

CHICKEN SOUP

By starting with a rich broth, this soup comes together in less than 15 minutes. It is flavored with Italian herbs and thickened instantly with a handful of couscous.

PREP TIME: 5 minutes	COOKING TIME: about 10 minutes	STORE: for up to 2 days, covered in the refrigerator. Reheat gently over low heat.	*Makes* **4** *servings*

» **1 tsp extra-virgin olive oil**

» **8 oz/225 g white mushrooms, brushed cleaned and sliced**

» **1 garlic clove, minced**

» **2 tsp Homemade Italian Seasoning (recipe follows)**

» **One 14½-oz/415-g can crushed tomatoes**

» **2 qt/2 l Old Chicken Broth (facing page)**

» **1 tbsp chopped fresh flat-leaf parsley**

» **¼ cup/50 g whole-wheat couscous**

Heat the olive oil in a large saucepan over medium-high heat until fragrant, about 30 seconds. Add the mushrooms and sauté until they soften, about 2 minutes. Stir in the garlic and the Italian seasoning and sauté until fragrant, another 10 seconds.

Add the tomatoes and Old Chicken Broth and simmer for 5 minutes. Add the parsley and couscous and stir to combine. Remove from the heat and let stand for 2 minutes to allow the couscous to plump, then serve hot.

Homemade Italian Seasoning

Although there are many Italian seasonings on the market, I manufacture a line of seasoning blends that I prefer.

Makes ¼ cup/30 g

» **1 tbsp dried thyme leaves**

» **1 tbsp dried basil leaves**

» **1½ tsp crushed dried rosemary leaves**

» **1 tsp dried marjoram leaves**

» **1 tsp rubbed sage**

» **2 tsp coarse sea salt**

» **½ teaspoon freshly ground black pepper**

Mix together the thyme, basil, rosemary, marjoram, sage, salt, and black pepper. Store for up to 1 month in a closed container in a dark cabinet.

Old Chicken Broth

Mature chickens are tough and wizened, but what they lack in youthful beauty they make up for in exquisite chickeny flavor—just what you want for broth. Also sold as stewing hens, these birds are usually chickens that have aged out of their egg-laying years. They tend to be small and dark-meated, and unsuitable for roasting or frying—which is why they are always on sale. They are more commonly available in ethnic markets. Make the broth in big batches, as it will have dozens of uses, and has such vibrant flavor it can be turned almost instantly into a delicious sauce. The soup can be served on its own, embellished with cooked noodles or rice.

Makes about 4 qt /3.8 l

» **2 stewing hens, about 2 lb/910 g each**
» **2 tsp fine sea salt**
» **12 fresh flat-leaf parsley sprigs**
» **12 peppercorns**
» **2 tsp dried thyme**
» **2 whole cloves**
» **4 large celery stalks, cut into 1-in/2.5-cm chunks**
» **2 large Spanish onions, cut into 1-in/2.5-cm chunks**
» **3 large carrots, peeled and cut into 1-in/2.5-cm chunks**

Wash the chickens well inside and out and rub with salt; set aside for 20 minutes.

Put the chickens in a large stockpot and add enough water to cover the birds by about 2 in/5 cm. Bring to a boil over medium heat. As the water reaches a boil, a layer of gray foam will form on the surface. Immediately reduce the heat so the water gently simmers and skim off the foam with a large spoon; discard it. Cover the pot partially, leaving the lid slightly ajar, and simmer until the stock tastes strongly of chicken, about 4 hours.

Put the parsley sprigs, peppercorns, thyme, and cloves in a square of cheesecloth and tie into a bouquet garni with kitchen string. Add to the pot along with the celery, onions, and carrots. Simmer until the broth is very full flavored, about 4 hours longer.

Strain the broth into a bowl through a colander, reserving both the solids and the liquid. Remove the skin and bones and the herb sachet; discard. Cut or tear the chicken meat into bite-size pieces and return to the broth with the vegetables. Store for up to 1 week, covered tightly in the refrigerator, or freeze for up to 3 months.

CHICKEN SOUP

Easily and instantly flavored with bottled Asian sauces that provide authentic zip right off the shelf, this bright and spicy soup is ready in less than 10 minutes.

PREP TIME: about 5 minutes	COOKING TIME: about 10 minutes	STORE: for up to 1 day, covered in the refrigerator. Reheat gently over low heat.	Makes **4** servings

» **2 qt/2 l Old Chicken Broth (page 91)**

» **2 tbsp soy sauce**

» **2 tbsp sherry wine vinegar**

» **2 tbsp Thai fish sauce**

» **1 tsp tomato paste**

» **2 tsp Sriracha hot chili sauce**

» **6 green onions, whites and tender green parts, thinly sliced**

» **Juice of ½ lemon**

In a large saucepan over medium-high heat, combine the broth, soy sauce, vinegar, fish sauce, and tomato paste and stir to mix well.

Bring to a simmer, then stir in the chili sauce, green onions, and lemon juice. Serve immediately.

TURKEY CHILI

Chili isn't simple. Though the stew is easy to prepare and as unpretentious as anything one can ladle into a bowl, the balance of flavors in a great chili are overwhelmingly complex. The sum of any chili is greater than any of its parts. Once you taste this slow-cooked version, with a beautiful blend of spices, any preconceptions you once had about American food being bland are forever banned. By lowering the temperature and lengthening the cooking time, the meat practically melts into the sauce, making an exceptionally smooth and rich mixture.

PREP TIME: 15 minutes	COOKING TIME: 4 to 8 hours	STORE: for up to 3 days, covered in the refrigerator. Reheat gently in a low oven or over low heat.	Makes **6** servings

» 2 tbsp vegetable oil

» 1 large Spanish onion, chopped

» 1 fresh long red chile or serrano chile, seeded and minced

» 1 garlic clove, minced

» 2 lb/910 g ground turkey

» Coarse sea salt and freshly ground black pepper

» 1 tbsp ground cumin seed

» 1 tsp dried oregano, preferably Mexican

» 2 tbsp chili powder

» ¼ cup/35 g cornmeal

» 1 qt/960 ml Old Chicken Broth (page 91)

» One 28-oz/800-g can crushed tomatoes

» 1 tbsp unsweetened cocoa powder

» Two 15-oz/430-g cans small white, black, or red beans, drained and rinsed

» ¼ cup/10 g chopped fresh cilantro

Preheat the oven to 200°F/95°C.

In a large Dutch oven, heat the oil over medium heat. Add the onion and sauté until it softens, about 4 minutes. Add the chile and garlic and sauté briefly until aromatic, about 30 seconds. Add the turkey and season generously with salt and pepper. Sauté, chopping and scraping with a spatula to separate the chunks of ground meat and to help it cook evenly.

When the turkey is mostly cooked, add the cumin, oregano, chili powder, and cornmeal and cook, stirring constantly, until the mixture is aromatic, about 3 minutes. Add the chicken broth, tomatoes, and cocoa powder. Stir until the mixture simmers and the cocoa dissolves. Stir in the beans and cover the pot. Transfer to the oven and cook until the meat is very soft and the flavors are very fragrant, 4 to 8 hours.

Just before serving, taste and adjust the seasoning with salt and pepper. Stir in the cilantro and serve.

VARIATION: IN A SLOW COOKER
Follow the recipe, but transfer the chili to a 6-qt/5.7-l slow cooker after the beans are added. Cook on low for 5 to 7 hours.

FETTUCCINE WITH
LAMB BOLOGNESE

Bolognese meat sauce is emblematic of the cooking of Bologna, known for slow-simmering braises and casseroles in which meat, vegetables, and cheese are combined with a kind of life-affirming joy and dreamy, comforting richness. And the amazing part is that the complex sauces are largely labor-free. You just combine the simple ingredients and let time in a warm oven work its magic.

CHILLING TIME: 40 minutes **PREP TIME:** 30 minutes	**COOKING TIME:** 4 to 6 hours	**STORE:** for up to 3 days, covered in the refrigerator. Rewarm gently in a low oven or over low heat.	*Makes* **4** TO **6** *servings*

» 4 lb/1.8 kg lamb shoulder, cut into 1-in/2.5-cm chunks

» 1 lb/455 g pork fatback, cut into ½-in/12-mm chunks

» 1 large Spanish onion, halved lengthwise and thinly sliced crosswise

» 1 large carrot, peeled and finely chopped

» 2 cups/480 ml dry red wine

» 2 qt/2 l water

» 6 fresh thyme sprigs

» 2 fresh rosemary sprigs

» 1 garlic clove

» 1 bay leaf

» ¼ cup/8 g dried mushrooms

» 1 cup/240 ml Simple Tomato Sauce (recipe follows) or good-quality store-bought tomato sauce

» Coarse sea salt and freshly ground black pepper

» 1 lb/455 g fresh fettuccine or 12 oz/340 g dried fettuccine

» 4 tbsp/55 g unsalted butter

» 1 cup/115 g freshly grated Parmesan cheese, preferably Parmigiano-Reggiano

Spread the lamb and fatback in a single layer on a baking sheet or other shallow pan that will fit into your freezer and freeze until firm but not solid, about 40 minutes. Grind the cold meat and fatback with a meat grinder, or pulse in a food processor in small batches. Try not to chop the meat too finely; you don't want a meat purée.

Preheat the oven to 250°F/120°C/gas ½.

Heat a large Dutch oven or large, deep cast-iron skillet over medium-high heat. Add the ground meat and cook until it is no longer red, stirring and scraping the bottom of the pan to cook the meat evenly, about 8 minutes. Add the onion and carrot and cook until barely tender, about 5 minutes.

Add the wine, scraping the bottom of the pan to mix any brown bits into the liquid and bring to a boil. Add the water and heat to simmering.

Meanwhile, put the thyme and rosemary sprigs, garlic clove, and bay leaf in a square of cheesecloth and tie into a bouquet garni with kitchen string. Add to the pot, along with the mushrooms and tomato sauce. Season with salt and pepper. Cover, transfer to the oven, and braise until the flavors are rich and blended, 4 to 6 hours. Discard the bouquet garni.

When the sauce is ready, cook the pasta (see Cooking and Saucing Pasta box, page 77).

CONTINUED

Transfer the sauce back to the stove top and to a simmer over medium-high heat. Stir in the butter and a ladleful of the reserved pasta-cooking water and simmer until the sauce is creamy. If the sauce gets too thick, add more pasta water, a little at a time, to reach the desired consistency. Add the cooked pasta and the Parmesan; toss to combine and serve immediately.

VARIATION: IN A SLOW COOKER
After starting the sauce on the stovetop, pour it into a 6-qt/5.7-l slow cooker and cook for 6 hours on low.

Simple Tomato Sauce

Tomato sauce, even a slow-cooked tomato sauce, does not benefit from hours on the stove. Cook just enough to make the tomatoes collapse into a sauce; any longer is overkill, producing a tomato sauce that is overly tart with a roasted caramelized flavor that undermines the fresh quality of the vegetables.

Makes about 6 cups/1.4 l

» **2 tbsp olive oil**
» **1 medium onion, finely chopped**
» **1 garlic clove, minced**
» **Two 28-oz/800-g cans crushed tomatoes**
» **2 tbsp extra-virgin olive oil**
» **Fine sea salt and freshly ground black pepper**

Heat the olive oil in a Dutch oven or large saucepan over medium heat. Add the onion and sauté until translucent, about 4 minutes. Add the garlic and cook until aromatic, about 1 minute. Add the tomatoes. Bring to a simmer, then reduce the heat to low, cover, and simmer very gently for 1 hour.

Remove from the heat. Stir in the extra-virgin olive oil and season with salt and pepper. Store for up to 3 days, covered in the refrigerator.

PORK AND SHRIMP

POSOLE

This Mexican-style pork stew, chock-full of hominy, chiles, tomatoes, lime juice, and cilantro, is garnished with shrimp in the last minutes of cooking. Long slow simmering is not appropriate for all ingredients. The pork shoulder is tenderized and enriched, bubbling away slowly in broth, but the shrimp need only a few minutes in the hot liquid to reach perfection. So that's what we do.

PREP TIME: 20 minutes	COOKING TIME: about 6 hours	STORE: for up to 2 days, covered in the refrigerator. Reheat gently in a low oven or over low heat.	*Makes* **6** *servings*

- » ¼ cup/30 g all-purpose flour
- » Fine sea salt and freshly ground black pepper
- » 2½ lb/1.2 kg boneless pork shoulder (picnic ham), trimmed of most of the exterior fat and cut into 1-in/2.5-cm cubes
- » 2 to 3 tbsp olive oil
- » 1 medium Spanish onion, chopped
- » 1 small red bell pepper, seeded and chopped
- » 1 fresh long red chile or serrano chile, seeded and minced
- » 1 garlic clove, minced
- » 1 cup/240 ml good-quality low-sodium chicken broth or fish broth (a good-quality fish boullion cube such as Knorr dissolved in boiling water works fine)
- » One 15-oz/430-g can diced tomatoes, with juice
- » One 15-oz/430-g can *posole* (whole hominy), drained and rinsed
- » 12 oz/340 g large (26-30 count) shrimp, peeled and deveined
- » Finely grated zest and juice of 1 lime
- » ¾ cup/30 g chopped fresh cilantro

Preheat the oven to 200°F/95°C.

Mix together the flour, 1 tsp salt, and ½ tsp pepper on a sheet of aluminum foil. Toss the pork pieces in the seasoned flour to coat completely.

In a large Dutch oven, pour enough olive oil to coat the bottom generously and place over medium-high heat. Heat until the oil is shimmering hot. Working in batches as needed to avoid crowding the pot, add the pork to the hot oil and cook to brown nicely on all sides, about 5 minutes per batch. Transfer the pork pieces to a plate as they are finished. When all of the pork is browned, set aside. Do not discard the remaining flour mixture.

If the pot seems dry, add more olive oil and return to medium-high heat. Add the onion and bell pepper and sauté until the vegetables soften, about 5 minutes. Add the chile and garlic and sauté until the garlic is aromatic, about 30 seconds more.

Add the reserved flour mixture and stir until dissolved in the oil in the pot. Cook, stirring constantly, until the flour toasts lightly, about 1 minute. Add the broth and the tomatoes with their juices and stir to mix well. Return to a simmer and season with more salt and pepper, if needed. Return the pork to the pot, along with any juices that accumulated on the plate. Stir in the *posole*. Cover, transfer to the oven, and cook until the flavors have blended and the pork is fork-tender, about 6 hours.

CONTINUED

Remove the pot from the oven, uncover, and stir in the shrimp and lime juice and zest. Re-cover and set aside and let the shrimp cook in the steam until firm and opaque throughout, about 2 minutes. Stir in the cilantro and serve.

VARIATION: IN A SLOW COOKER

Follow the recipe, but cut the amount of broth in half. Cook in a 6-qt/5.7-l slow cooker on low for 5 to 7 hours. Add the shrimp, lime, and cilantro at the end as directed.

BOURBON-BACON BEANS

Baked beans come from an age when cooking food all day (or for several days) over a low fire or in a slow oven was commonplace. There was no sautéed boneless chicken breast or food processor pesto, and the cooks who baked those beans were plowing the fields to set the next crop while they cooked. Homemade baked beans stand at the apex of great slow-cooking recipes; while cooks of all stripes may say that canned baked beans are the best, making your own is a rare and unrivaled treat—and easy! Except for a few minutes of hands-on time, you can walk away until the sun goes down.

PREP TIME: 5 minutes	COOKING TIME: about 5 hours (mostly unattended)	STORE: for up to 1 week, covered in the refrigerator. Reheat gently over low heat or in a low oven.	Makes **12** servings

» 1 lb/455 g dried white beans such as great Northern (see Note)

» 8 oz/255 g bacon, finely diced

» 1 large yellow onion, finely diced

» 1 tbsp smoked paprika

» 1 tsp dried thyme

» 1 tsp dried oregano

» 2 tsp coarse sea salt

» ½ tsp freshly ground black pepper

» ½ tsp red pepper flakes

» 3 garlic cloves, minced

» 2 bay leaves

» One 14½-oz/415-g can diced tomatoes, with juice

» ½ cup/120 ml molasses

» ⅓ cup/65 g sugar

» 2 cups/480 ml Old Chicken Broth (page 91)

» ½ cup/120 ml bourbon

» 2 tbsp brown mustard

» 1 tbsp soy sauce

Pick over the beans for stones or grit. Rinse in a colander and drain well. Put the beans in a Dutch oven and add water to cover by about 3 in/7.5 cm. Bring to a boil over high heat, then reduce the heat to medium-low and cook until rehydrated, about 1½ hours. A bean cut in half should be moist all the way through. Drain and set aside.

Put the Dutch oven back over medium-low heat. Add the bacon and cook until the fat renders out, about 15 minutes. Don't rush it; the bacon should be cooked but not crisp.

Add the onion, paprika, thyme, oregano, salt, black pepper, and red pepper flakes and cook until the onion is tender and the spices are aromatic, about 10 minutes. Add the garlic and bay leaves and cook for 1 minute longer.

Add the tomatoes, molasses, sugar, chicken broth, bourbon, mustard, and soy sauce; stir to mix well; and bring to a simmer. Add the cooked beans, cover, and reduce the heat to low. Simmer until tender and flavorful, about 3 hours. Serve immediately, or let cool, refrigerate overnight, and reheat gently to serve the next day, after the flavors have deepened even more.

NOTE: *For a shortcut, substitute four 15-oz/430-g cans white beans, rinsed and drained, for the cooked dried beans.*

GOULASH

Goulashes are meat-and-onion soup-stews from Hungary. They are typically very plain, seasoned only with paprika and occasionally some caraway—never Frenchified with wine nor Germanicized with beer. They may have a little tomato and some hot pepper to spice things up; but they are *always* slow-cooked. Whether buried in hot coals in a cast-iron casserole, shoved into a slow oven, or parked on a low back burner, goulash takes its time to relax, while the ample amount of onions cooks into a syrupy mass. The effect is luxurious, belly-warming, and delicious. Serve with boiled or mashed potatoes. The use of lard is traditional for *gulyás*, but I often use butter.

PREP TIME: 10 minutes	**COOKING TIME: 4 to 6 hours**	**STORE:** for up to 1 week, covered in the refrigerator. Rewarm gently over low heat.	*Makes* **4** *servings*

- » 2 tbsp lard or unsalted butter
- » 3 lb/1.4 kg bone-in beef short ribs, cut into 2-in/5-cm chunks
- » 3 yellow onions, halved from stem to root end, then thinly sliced in the same direction
- » 1 garlic clove, peeled but left whole
- » 1 tsp caraway seeds
- » 1½ tsp coarse sea salt
- » 2 tbsp sweet paprika
- » 3 cups/720 ml warm water
- » 1 cup/185 g diced tomatoes, fresh or canned, with juice
- » Freshly ground black pepper

In a large Dutch oven over medium heat, melt the lard. Add the short ribs and sear just until golden brown on their meaty sides (the surface of the meat should not get too dark golden). Using tongs, transfer to a bowl.

Add the onions to the fat in the pot and toss to coat. Cover and cook until the onions soften, about 5 minutes.

Meanwhile, on a cutting board, stir together the garlic, caraway, and salt and chop and crush with the flat side of the knife blade until everything is uniformly finely chopped. Add to the onions along with the paprika and stir to combine. Stir in the warm water and tomatoes with their juices, season with pepper, and bring to a boil.

Put the short ribs, bone-side down, on top of the onions, and drizzle with any juices that accumulated in the bowl. Cover the pot and turn down the heat to achieve the lowest possible simmer. Simmer very gently until the meat is fork-tender and the onions have broken down to a coarse pulp, 4 to 6 hours. Serve hot.

VARIATION: IN A SLOW COOKER
Follow the recipe, but reduce the amount of water to 2¼ cups/ 540 ml. Cook in a 6-qt/5.7-l slow cooker on low for 6 hours.

POT ROAST

It is an odd quirk of bovine economics that the cheapest cuts of beef are also the most flavorful. That's because, in the meat world, increased flavor comes at the expense of tenderness (and tenderness is what beef prices are based on). Good news for slow cooking, where toughness is an asset rather than a deficit. Tender meats become dry and grainy during slow cooking, but give me a grizzled joint of chuck and I will turn it into succulent, flavor-packed pot roast every time.

SEASONING TIME: 1 hour **PREP TIME:** 10 minutes	**COOK TIME:** 4 to 6 hours on high, 8 to 10 hours on low	**STORE:** for up to 5 days covered in the refrigerator. Rewarm gently in a low oven or over low heat.	*Makes* **6** TO **8** *servings*

» 2 tbsp sweet paprika

» 1 tsp garlic powder

» 1 tbsp coarse sea salt

» ½ tsp coarsely ground black pepper

» 3 lb/1.4 kg boneless chuck roast, trimmed of excess fat

» 2 tbsp olive oil

» 1 large onion, chopped

» 1 cup/240 ml vegetable cocktail juice, such as V8

» ½ cup/120 ml apple juice

» ⅓ cup/75 ml apple cider vinegar

» ½ cup/100 g firmly packed brown sugar

Mix the paprika, garlic powder, salt, and pepper in a small bowl. Rub all over the meat, wrap in plastic wrap, and rest for 1 hour.

Heat 1 tbsp of the oil in a large frying pan over medium-high heat. Brown the roast on all sides, starting fatty-side down. Transfer to a 6-qt/5.7-l slow cooker.

Add the remaining 1 tbsp olive oil to the frying pan. Add the onion and cook until browned, about 3 minutes. Add the vegetable juice, apple juice, vinegar, and brown sugar, and bring to a boil. Pour over the meat and cook on high for 4 to 6 hours or on low for 8 to 10 hours, until the meat is fork-tender.

Transfer the roast to a cutting board. Skim the fat from the surface of the juices in the cooker. Heat the juices on high for 10 minutes while the meat rests. Slice the roast against the grain and arrange the slices overlapping on a large platter. Ladle enough sauce over top to moisten; serve remaining sauce on the side.

BEEF BRISKET

WITH PRUNES AND ORANGES

I am pretty sure I have several admirable accomplishments to my credit in this life, but the perfection of this brisket recipe is the one I am currently most proud of. It really is stellar! The meat is rubbed with coffee and cinnamon, which alone would give it a roasted redolence; but after that, the brisket simmers and browns with brandy, caramelized onions, orange zest, and prunes for almost half a day, and emerges inundated with sweet beefiness. The amount of gravy is intentionally abundant, so you will have plenty for dipping bread into, splashing over noodles, or eating by the spoonful.

CHILLING TIME: at least 1 hour and up to overnight **PREP TIME:** 20 minutes	**COOKING TIME:** 6½ to 10½ hours	**STORE:** for up to 5 days, covered in the refrigerator. Rewarm gently in a low oven.	*Makes* **8** *servings*

» ¼ cup/20 g finely ground coffee

» 1 tsp ground cinnamon

» 4 tsp sea salt

» 1 tsp freshly ground black pepper

» 3 lb/1.4 kg beef brisket, trimmed of excess fat

» 2 tbsp vegetable oil

» 2 large Spanish onions, cut into thin wedges

» 8 celery stalks, cut into 1-in/ 2.5-cm pieces

» 4 garlic cloves, minced

» ¼ cup/60 ml brandy

» ½ cup/120 ml cider vinegar

» 6 tbsp/65 g firmly packed dark brown sugar

» 2 cups/480 ml vegetable cocktail juice, such as V8

» Juice and julienned zest of 2 oranges

» 16 pitted prunes

Mix together the coffee grounds, cinnamon, salt, and pepper in a small bowl. Rub half of the mixture all over the brisket. Refrigerate for at least 1 hour and up to overnight.

Preheat the oven to 200°F/95°C.

Heat 1 tbsp of the oil in a large Dutch oven over high heat. Add the brisket and sear until nicely browned on both sides, about 5 minutes per side. Transfer to a plate.

Add the remaining 1 tbsp oil to the pot. Add the onions and celery and sauté until lightly browned, about 8 minutes. Add the garlic and sauté just until aromatic, about 1 minute more. Add the brandy and bring to a boil. Add the vinegar, brown sugar, vegetable juice, and the remaining coffee mixture and return to a boil. Add the orange juice and zest, the prunes, and any meat juices that accumulated on the plate. Return the brisket to the pot and spoon the liquid in the pot over to submerge the meat. Cover and transfer to the oven. Braise until the meat can be pierced easily with a fork, 6 to 10 hours.

Using two large forks, transfer the brisket to a cutting board and let rest for 15 minutes. Carve the brisket crosswise against the grain into thin slices and arrange the slices on a platter. Spoon the sauce and braised vegetables over and around the brisket and serve.

BOUILLON-POACHED
ᨠ BEEF CHUCK ᨠ
WITH GREEN-APPLE SLAW

I confess: I was not a fan of poached beef. The leanness of the technique and the richness of the ingredient strike me as discordant. And so I was surprised—elated, even—by the delicious results of this experiment. The tough hunk of beef chuck emerged from its poaching liquid as tender as a filet steak; the extra long and low cooking pushed the potentially bland tradition into a whole different, and unusually sublime, rendition of meat cooked in a simmering liquid. And the resulting broth made amazing beef soup the next night. (You should have 3 to 4 cups/720 to 960 ml of leftover broth from this recipe.)

CHILLING TIME: 12 to 24 hours PREP TIME: 20 minutes	COOKING TIME: about 6 hours	STORE: for up to 5 days, covered in the refrigerator. Rewarm gently in a low oven.	*Makes* **8** *servings*

» 3 lb/1.4 kg boneless beef chuck

» 1 tsp coarse sea salt

» 1 tsp freshly ground black pepper

» 1 tsp dried thyme

» 1 tsp vegetable oil

» 2 medium carrots, peeled and thinly sliced

» 2 celery stalks, thinly sliced

» 1 medium yellow onion, chopped

» ½ cup/120 ml dry red wine

» ¼ cup/60 ml red wine vinegar

» 2 cups/480 ml good-quality low-sodium beef broth

» 1 tbsp tomato paste

FOR THE GREEN-APPLE SLAW:

» 2 large green apples, such as Granny Smith, scrubbed and cored but unpeeled

» 4 celery stalks, scrubbed and tough strings removed

» 2 tbsp mayonnaise

» 1 tbsp apple cider vinegar

» 1 tsp whole-grain mustard

» Sea salt and freshly ground black pepper

Season the meat with the salt, pepper, and thyme. Put on a rack set on a rimmed baking sheet and refrigerate, uncovered, for at least 12 hours and up to 24 hours.

Remove the meat from the refrigerator an hour before you plan to start cooking. Preheat the oven to 200°F/95°C.

In a large Dutch oven over medium heat, heat the oil. When the oil is hot, add the carrots, celery, and onion and toss to coat with the oil. Cover and cook, stirring occasionally, until the vegetables start to release their juices, about 5 minutes. Raise the heat to medium-high and add the wine. Bring to a boil. Add the vinegar, broth, and tomato paste and stir to mix well. When the liquid returns to a simmer, put the beef in the pot. Cover, transfer to the oven, and cook until very tender, about 6 hours.

While the meat is cooking, make the slaw: Shred the apple and celery on the biggest holes of a box grater-shredder or in a food processor fitted with the shredding blade. Put the slaw in a large bowl.

In a small bowl, combine the mayonnaise, vinegar, and mustard, season with salt and pepper, and stir to mix well. Fold the mayonnaise mixture into the shredded apple and celery. Cover and refrigerate until ready to serve.

Carve the beef crosswise against the grain into thin slices. Arrange the slices on plates and moisten with some of the cooking liquid. Serve with the slaw on the side.

VARIATION: IN A SLOW COOKER

Follow the recipe, but after making the poaching liquid, arrange everything in a 6-qt/5.7-l slow cooker. Cook for 4 to 5 hours on high or 6 to 8 hours on low.

VARIATION: PULLED BEEF SANDWICHES

Using two forks, shred the cooked beef chuck. Moisten with some of the cooking liquid. Serve on split soft rolls such as hamburger buns, topped with a dollop of apple slaw.

VARIATION: BEEF AND RICE SOUP

In a saucepan over medium-high heat, combine 2 tbsp white rice, 1 peeled and sliced carrot, 1 diced tomato, 1 sliced celery stalk, and 3 to 4 cups/720 to 960 ml of the broth left over from poaching the beef. Bring to a simmer. Cook until the rice and vegetables are tender, about 12 minutes. Add some chopped leftover meat and season with salt and pepper. *Makes 2 servings.*

CORNED BEEF–
STUFFED CABBAGE

Corned beef and cabbage takes so long to cook, and is such a big deal to prepare, it seems like I am always slightly disappointed that after all is said and done, it is never anything more than . . . corned beef and cabbage. Since I feel similarly about stuffed cabbage, I decided to try combining the underachievers into something that might seem better worth the effort. Success! Without a lot more work, the results are way more impressive.

Slow cooking is a great way to ensure a tender turn on this classic dish with less labor—and because neither the stuffed cabbage nor the corned beef is easily overcooked, you can stretch the simmering time without sacrificing quality. Choose a cabbage with tightly wrapped, bright green leaves.

PREP TIME: 45 minutes	COOKING TIME: about 6 hours	STORE: for up to 5 days, covered in the refrigerator. Rewarm gently in a low oven.	*Makes* **10** *servings*

» 1 large head green cabbage, about 2½ lb/1.2 kg

» 2 corned beef briskets, each about 2½ lb/1.2 kg

» 2 large yellow onions, each cut into 8 chunks

» ½ cup/55 g dried bread crumbs

» ½ cup/100 g white rice

» 1 tsp dried thyme

» 3 cups/720 ml dark beer

» 1 cup/240 ml ketchup

» 1 tsp sea salt

» ¾ tsp freshly ground black pepper

» 1 bay leaf

Bring a big pot of water to a boil. Remove the entire core of the cabbage with a paring knife. Immerse the head of cabbage in the boiling water for 3 minutes. Remove all of the outer leaves that have become flexible. Repeat until you have 20 good-size leaves for stuffing.

Slice one of the corned beef briskets thinly, then chop finely. Chop four of the onion chunks finely. Grind the chopped corned beef and chopped onion with a meat grinder, or pulse in a food processor in small batches. Try not to chop the meat too finely; you don't want a meat purée. Put the beef and onion mixture in a bowl. Add the bread crumbs, rice, and thyme.

Remove the hard triangular rib from the base of each cabbage leaf. Spoon about ⅓ cup/40 g of the filling in an oval mound near the end of each leaf where the rib was and roll up toward the far edge, tucking the sides in as you roll.

Arrange the remaining onion pieces in the bottom of a large Dutch oven. Put the other corned beef on top of the onions and nestle the cabbage rolls, seam-side down, around the corned beef.

In a bowl, stir together the beer, ketchup, salt, and pepper and pour into the pot. Tuck in the bay leaf. Place over medium heat and bring to a boil. Reduce the heat to maintain a bare simmer (make sure the heat is as low as possible), cover, and cook slowly until the corned beef is easily pierced with a fork, about 6 hours.

Discard the bay leaf. Lift the corned beef onto a cutting board and cut into slices crosswise against the grain. Arrange a few slices on each plate and tuck a stuffed cabbage roll or two alongside. Moisten everything with some of the cooking liquid and serve.

VARIATION: IN A SLOW COOKER
Follow the recipe, but instead of arranging the onion chunks, whole corned beef, and stuffed cabbage rolls in a Dutch oven, layer them in a 6-qt/5.7-l slow cooker. Reduce the beer to 2 cups/480 ml and the ketchup to ¾ cup/180 ml. Cook for 4 to 5 hours on high, or 8 to 10 hours on low.

VEAL TONGUE

Counterintuitive though it may seem, good-tasting meat comes from well-exercised muscles. Though we associate exercise with arms and legs and abs and chests, there are few muscles in anyone's body that get a better workout than the tongue, and this holds true for cows, for which cud chewing is a daily activity that approaches Olympic training levels.

The idea of eating tongue is sometimes challenging for some eaters, even meat eaters— even bold ones; but once you get over the fact of it, tongue is very similar in flavor to other muscle meats, and slow cooking is the perfect way to experience its delicate consistency. Veal tongues are small and available from any good butcher. If you have trouble finding them, you can substitute one beef tongue for the two veal tongues. The cooking time doesn't change.

CHILLING TIME: 8 to 24 hours PREP TIME: 20 minutes	COOKING TIME: 6 to 8 hours	STORE: for up to 3 days, covered in the refrigerator. Rewarm gently in a low oven or over low heat.	*Makes* **6** *servings*

» 2 veal tongues, about 1 lb/455 g each

» 1 tsp fine sea salt

» ½ tsp freshly ground black pepper

» 1 tbsp olive oil

» 2 medium carrots, peeled and finely diced

» 1 large celery stalk, finely diced

» 1 medium yellow onion, finely diced

» ⅓ cup/75 ml vegetable cocktail juice, such as V8

» 3 tbsp apple cider vinegar

» 1 tbsp soy sauce

» 2 tbsp dark brown sugar

» 2 tbsp chopped fresh flat-leaf parsley

Rub the tongues all over with the salt and pepper and refrigerate, uncovered, for at least 8 hours and up to 24 hours.

Preheat the oven to 200°F/95°C.

In a large cast-iron skillet, heat the olive oil over medium-high heat. Add the carrots, celery, and onion to the hot oil and sauté until lightly browned, about 5 minutes. Remove from the heat. Arrange the veal tongues on the bed of sautéed vegetables.

In a small bowl, whisk together the vegetable juice, vinegar, soy sauce, and brown sugar until the sugar dissolves. Pour over the tongues. Cover the pan with heavy-duty aluminum foil and braise until the tongues are easily pierced with a fork, 6 to 8 hours.

Remove from the oven and transfer the tongues to a cutting board. Stir the parsley into the pan juices to make a sauce. Make a small slit on one end of each tongue. Grab the skin near the slit with tongs or your fingers and peel the skin from the tongues like removing a stocking. Discard the skin.

Cut the tongues crosswise into thin slices and arrange on a platter. Spoon the sweet-and-sour sauce in the pan over top. Serve immediately.

VARIATION: IN A SLOW COOKER

Put the sautéed vegetables in a 4-qt/3.5-l slow cooker. Assemble the remaining ingredients in the slow cooker, cover, and cook for 6 to 8 hours on low.

BABY OCTOPUS
SIMMERED IN TOMATILLO SOFRITO

Similar to squid, octopus can be cooked long and slow until it becomes melt-in-your-mouth tender. This slow-cooked rendition epitomizes this esthetic. The octopi are simmered with a simple mélange of vegetables called a *sofrito*, a combination of tomatoes (in this case tomatillos), onion, and chiles. I used serranos and added a dose of lime to reinforce the citrusy tang of the tomatillos.

Most adult octopus is sold frozen and already cleaned, weighing between 2 and 4 lb/910 g and 1.8 kg. Baby octopi are frequently available "fresh," although these have most likely been previously frozen. If you cringe at the thought of buying frozen seafood, relax; freezing (usually that means flash freezing on the fishing boat the day of the catch) is beneficial to tough-muscled seafood like octopus and squid, making them tenderize more easily during cooking, and it does nothing to compromise their flavor.

PREP TIME: 10 minutes	**COOKING TIME:** 2½ to 3 hours	**STORE:** for up to 3 days, covered in the refrigerator. Reheat gently in a low oven.	*Makes* **4** TO **6** *servings*

» **16 tomatillos**

» **6 tbsp/90 ml olive oil**

» **1 medium yellow onion, quartered lengthwise and thinly sliced crosswise**

» **2 lb/910 g cleaned baby octopi**

» **1 jalapeño or serrano chile, seeded and minced**

» **Coarse sea salt and freshly ground black pepper**

» **Juice of 1 large lime**

» **Small handful of chopped fresh flat-leaf parsley**

» **Slow-Fried Potatoes (page 153) for serving (optional)**

Preheat the oven to 200°F/95°C.

Remove the papery skins from the tomatillos and rinse under warm running water to dissolve the sticky coating on the fruit. Dice finely and set aside.

In a large Dutch oven or cast-iron skillet, heat 3 tbsp of the olive oil over medium heat. Add the onion and sauté until it softens, about 5 minutes. Add the octopi and chile and stir until the octopi feel firm and their tentacles curl.

Add the tomatillos, season with salt and pepper, and stir to mix well. Cover the pan with a lid or heavy-duty aluminum foil and bake until the octopi are fork-tender, 2½ to 3 hours.

Stir in the lime juice, parsley, and the remaining 3 tbsp olive oil. Taste and adjust the seasoning. Serve immediately on a bed of fried potatoes, if desired.

VARIATION: IN A SLOW COOKER

To make octopus in a slow cooker, prepare the recipe in a skillet until you add the tomatillos. Put the tomatillos and salt and pepper in a 4- to 6-qt/3.5- to 5.7-l slow cooker. Scrape and pour the sautéed ingredients over the top. Cover and cook on low for 6 hours.

CHAPTER 4

· SLOW ·

STEAMING

Steaming and simmering are companion cooking techniques. Both cook with moving moisture. The major difference is that steam is a bit more energetic than simmering water and therefore can permeate food faster and more deeply, provided that it is contained. It can also overcook ingredients, especially proteins, if it is not carefully controlled.

Ideally, for most slow steaming, the liquid should stay just below a simmer at about 180°F/82°C. At that temperature, the surface of the water is just beginning to wobble, whiffs of steam rise periodically, and a few bubbles may appear near the edge of the pan. It is liquid on the verge of turning into gas. Your job is to keep it from transitioning completely.

Steaming can be done in a perforated steaming basket set above a pot of pre-simmering liquid or with minimal liquid in a covered baking dish set in a warm (200°F/95°C) oven. When cooked with care, slow-steamed food can be incredibly delicious, subtly scented with simmering herbs, spices, teas, and/or aromatic vegetables.

Although it is most common to think of delicate ingredients—lean fish, spring vegetables, eggs—as candidates for steaming, I have found that slow steaming works wonders on tough gnarly meats and fibrous pungent vegetables, softening and smoothing out their harsh edges.

BROWN BREAD

Not much more than a century ago, it was still fairly unusual for people to have ovens in their homes, so baking was typically done either in a Dutch oven by the side of the fire or in closed baking pans, also called molds, set in a pot of simmering water. Steamed breads and puddings are one of the last vestiges of this type of cooking still performed in modern kitchens.

You will need a few specialty pieces of equipment for this recipe: a 2-qt/2-l bread mold, pudding mold, or soufflé dish, or two 13- to 16-oz/370- to 455-g coffee cans and baking rings or trivets to support them (you can also use empty tuna cans with both ends cut off or canning jar rings).

PREP TIME: 15 minutes	COOKING TIME: about 2½ hours	STORE: Best eaten within a few hours.	*Makes* **4** *servings*

» Vegetable oil spray
» 1 cup/130 g rye flour
» 1 cup/140 g blue cornmeal
» 1 cup/130 g whole-wheat flour
» 2 tsp ground ginger
» 1 tsp ground cinnamon
» ½ tsp dry mustard
» ¼ tsp ground allspice
» ⅛ tsp ground cloves
» 2 tsp baking soda
» 1 tsp fine sea salt
» 2 cups/340 g raisins
» 1 cup/240 ml black coffee
» 1 cup/240 ml yogurt
» ¾ cup/180 ml molasses
» Boiling water as needed
» Unsalted butter for serving (optional)

Coat the inside of the bread mold(s) lightly with vegetable oil spray; set aside.

In a large bowl, whisk together the rye flour, cornmeal, whole-wheat flour, ginger, cinnamon, mustard, allspice, cloves, baking soda, and salt. Toss in the raisins to coat. In a separate bowl, beat together the coffee, yogurt, and molasses, and then stir the yogurt mixture into the dry ingredients just until a smooth batter forms.

Pour the batter into the prepared mold(s). Cover the top of the mold(s) with heavy-duty aluminum foil and secure around the top with kitchen string or a rubber band.

Position the baking ring(s) in a Dutch oven or saucepan wide and deep enough to hold the molds. Put the mold(s) on top of the ring(s) and pour boiling water around the mold(s) until the water comes about halfway up the sides but does not touch the foil. Cover the pot and steam the bread over low heat, adding more water if the level drops by more than half, until the top of the bread is dry and the center feels springy but soft, about 2½ hours.

Remove the mold(s) from the water and cool for 5 minutes. Take off the foil. Run a knife around the edge of the bread and invert onto a plate. Serve warm in slices with butter, if desired.

EGGS
BARELY STEAMED
OVER TOMATOES AND FRESH HERBS

The art of slow cooking, as you have presumably seen while eating your way through this book, centers tightly around the specific tenderness and toughness of different proteins, and how—and how greatly—they are affected by temperature. These phenomena are intensely in play when cooking eggs. You will recognize this science from watching an egg cook in hot butter in a skillet: egg white begins to thicken at 145°F/63°C, is tender-firm at 150°F/66°C, and is solid at 180°F/82°C. Yolk proteins begin to set at 150°F/66°C and are fully set at 158°F/70°C. A beaten egg sets at around 165°F/74°C. Because simmering water is 180°F/82°C, it is best to steam eggs well below a simmer to ensure that they stay tender.

This recipe, a variation on the perfect soft-boiled or poached egg, is a delicious test for the soft touch of slow cooking. Serve with thick slices of toast, if you like.

PREP TIME: 5 minutes	**COOKING TIME:** about 50 minutes	**STORE:** Best served immediately.	*Makes* **4** *servings*

- » 1 tbsp olive oil
- » ½ medium yellow onion, finely chopped
- » 1 garlic clove, minced
- » ½ cup/120 ml dry white wine
- » One 14½-oz/415-g can diced tomatoes, drained
- » Sea salt and freshly ground black pepper
- » 1 cup/30 g fresh herb leaves such as basil, dill, flat-leaf parsley, chive, thyme, rosemary, and/or mint, in any combination, finely chopped
- » 8 large eggs
- » Finely grated zest of ½ lemon

In a large skillet with a lid, heat the olive oil over medium heat. Add the onion and sauté until translucent, about 4 minutes. Add half of the garlic, stir twice, and add the white wine. Raise the heat to high and bring to a boil. Add the tomatoes and season with salt and pepper. Bring to a very gentle simmer, then turn the heat down; the liquid should just bubble around the edges of the pan and whiffs of steam should be rising from the center. Stir in half of the herbs. Keep the heat as low as possible.

Crack 2 eggs into a cup and carefully slide onto the surface of the tomatoes. Repeat in the same manner with the remaining eggs. Cover the pan and steam until the eggs are set, about 40 minutes.

While the eggs are steaming, combine the remaining herbs and garlic and the lemon zest; set aside.

To serve, using a large spoon, scoop a pair of eggs and the tomatoes beneath them onto a plate. Season with salt and pepper, and scatter some of the herb mixture over the top of each portion.

SAUSAGES
STEAMED IN PORTER BROTH

The dark malt used in brewing porter and stout lends a bittersweet molasses richness to this novel dish of steamed sausage. By laying the sausages on a bed of simmering vegetables, they gently steam from above, making it unlikely that they will overcook, even if the steaming time is extended. Although steaming directly over alcohol can lead to harsh fumes entering the food, the relatively low alcohol content of beer and the step of bringing the steaming liquid to a boil before adding the sausages ensure that the meat will absorb all of the sweet umami flavor of dark beer and none of its pungency.

Serve over noodles or mashed sweet potatoes.

PREP TIME: 5 minutes	COOKING TIME: about 2¼ hours	STORE: for up to 3 days, covered in the refrigerator. Reheat gently in a low oven.	*Makes* **4** *servings*

» 1 tbsp vegetable oil

» 8 sweet Italian sausages, about 1½ lb/680 g total weight

» 1 tbsp unsalted butter

» 2 large yellow onions, halved and thinly sliced

» 1 tbsp all-purpose flour

» 2 tsp light brown sugar

» 1 cup/240 ml good-quality low-sodium chicken or vegetable broth

» 1 cup/240 ml dark beer

Preheat the oven to 250°F/120°C/gas ½.

In a large, deep cast-iron skillet over medium-high heat, heat the oil. Add the sausages and cook until browned nicely on all sides, about 5 minutes total. Transfer the sausages to a plate.

Reduce the heat to medium. Add the butter and let melt, then add the onions and sauté until lightly browned, about 8 minutes. Stir in the flour and cook, stirring often, until lightly toasted, 3 or 4 minutes. Add the brown sugar, broth, and beer and bring to a boil. Cook for 1 minute. Lay the sausages on top of the bed of onions; they should be sitting in liquid about halfway up their sides. Drizzle in any juices that accumulated on the plate. Cover the pan tightly with a lid or a sheet of heavy-duty aluminum foil. Bake until the sausages are plump and the steaming liquid has thickened into a sauce, about 2 hours. Serve immediately.

GREENS AND BEANS

OVEN-STEAMED IN BACON AND BEER

Mature hearty leafy greens such as kale, collard, and mustard like to be well cooked. They are overtly bitter when raw and still acrid when al dente, but take the time to let them soften and they become sweet and rich tasting—sort of like stewed meat. This recipe for leafy greens steamed in beer with white beans is hearty enough to be served as a main dish, with bread or corn sticks alongside. And the slow cooking allows you to set them up well ahead of the kitchen rush.

PREP TIME: 10 minutes	**COOKING TIME:** about 2¼ hours	**STORE:** for up to 3 days, covered in refrigerator. Reheat gently in low oven or over low heat.	*Makes* **4** *servings*

» 3 bacon strips

» ½ yellow onion, finely chopped

» One 15½-oz/445-g can cannellini beans, rinsed and drained

» One 12-oz/360-ml bottle lager beer

» 1 large bunch kale, collard, or mustard greens, or a mixture (about 1½ lb/680 g), tough stems and center spines trimmed and discarded, cut into bite-size pieces

» Coarse sea salt and freshly ground black pepper

Preheat the oven to 200°F/95°C.

Cook the bacon in a large cast-iron skillet over medium heat until the pan is coated with a layer of bacon fat and the bacon is crisp, about 8 minutes. Transfer the bacon to paper towels to drain.

Add the onion to the pan and sauté until softened, about 3 minutes. Add the beans and beer and bring to a boil. Remove from the heat. Crumble the bacon over the beans. Pile the kale into the pan and season liberally with salt and pepper. Cover with a lid or a layer of heavy-duty aluminum foil and steam gently in the oven until the greens are tender and most of the liquid has evaporated, about 2 hours.

Uncover and toss everything together to mix well. Taste and adjust the seasoning, and serve immediately.

VARIATION: IN A SLOW COOKER

Combine the cooked bacon and onions in a 6-qt/5.7-l slow cooker. Add the remaining ingredients, reducing the beer by half (have a toast with the other half). Cook on low for 3 to 4 hours.

CORIANDER ❧ SPARE RIBS ❧
WITH CILANTRO BUTTER

More subtle than barbecue but equally as effective at tenderizing gnarly sinews and tough flesh, steaming is an excellent (and novel) way to prepare pork spare ribs. Pork rib racks can be butchered in several ways. One of the neatest, and the one I prefer, is known as the "St. Louis cut," in which all bones that keep the rack from having a clean rectangular appearance are trimmed away.

MARINATING TIME: 6 to 12 hours PREP TIME: 15 minutes	COOKING TIME: about 6 hours	STORE: for up to 3 days, covered in the refrigerator. Reheat gently in a low oven.	*Makes* **6** *servings*

» 3 tbsp ground coriander

» 2 tbsp raw sugar

» 1 tbsp ground cumin

» Sea salt and freshly ground black pepper

» Finely grated zest and juice of 2 limes

» ½ cup/20 g chopped fresh cilantro

» 2 racks of pork ribs, about 4 lb/ 1.8 kg each, preferably St. Louis cut

» 4 tbsp unsalted butter

» 1 garlic clove, minced

Combine the coriander, sugar, cumin, ¼ cup salt, 2 tsp pepper, and 2 cups/480 ml water in a large zippered plastic bag. Seal and shake until the sugar and salt dissolve. Open the bag and add half of the lime zest and juice and half of the cilantro. Cut the rib racks in half and put in the bag with the brine. Seal the bag again, but leave a corner open and push on the bag to make sure you release any trapped air through the opening. Close the zipper completely. Massage the liquid gently into the meat and refrigerate for at least 6 hours and up to 12 hours.

Preheat the oven to 200°F/95°C.

Put the ribs in on a rack in a large roasting pan. Pour enough of the brine from the bag into the pan so that it covers the bottom of the pan but doesn't touch the rib meat. Cover the pan with aluminum foil and steam until the rib meat is falling-off-the-bone tender, about 6 hours.

Raise the oven temperature to 450°F/230°C/gas 8, remove the foil, and bake until the ribs are browned, about 15 minutes.

While the ribs are browning, put the butter and garlic in a saucepan over medium heat and cook until the garlic sizzles, about 1 minute. Add the remaining lime zest and juice and bring to a boil. Remove from heat and stir in the remaining ¼ cup cilantro. Taste and adjust the seasoning with salt and pepper.

Cut the racks into individual ribs and serve drizzled with the cilantro butter.

GARLIC-GINGER
⋙ LOBSTER ⋘
SLOW-STEAMED OVER CHILES IN COCONUT MILK

This is a spectacularly beautiful dish. The bright red shells of the slow-steamed lobsters pick up flavor as well as color on the plate from fiery red chiles, with everything set off by flecks of fresh green cilantro swimming in a creamy bath of coconut milk. Tender Italian risotto-style Arborio rice steams with the coconut milk in the hollows of the lobsters, transforming into a sweet, nutty pudding that's a perfect complement to the rich meat. The results seem luxurious, exotic, and simple, all at once.

PREP TIME: 30 minutes	**COOKING TIME:** about 2 hours	**STORE:** Best served immediately.	*Makes* **4** *servings*

» 2 garlic cloves, minced

» One 2-in/5-cm piece fresh ginger, peeled and minced

» 4 tbsp Arborio rice

» 8 fresh long red chiles

» 2 large live lobsters, about 2 lb/ 910 g each, halved lengthwise and cleaned (see Working with Live Lobsters box, following)

» 1½ cups/360 ml coconut milk

» Grated zest and juice of 1 lime

» 1 tbsp dry sherry

» 1 tsp toasted sesame oil

» 2 tbsp chopped fresh cilantro

Preheat the oven to 225°F/110°C.

In a small bowl, stir together the garlic and ginger. Put the rice in another small bowl and add 1 teaspoon of the garlic-ginger mixture. Toss to mix well and set aside.

Arrange the chiles parallel to one another across the bottom of a baking dish. Put the lobster halves, cut-side up, in a single layer on the rack of chiles. Carefully spoon 1 tbsp of the rice mixture into the cavity of each lobster half. Spoon 2 tbsp of the coconut milk into each cavity and spread gently to moisten the rice. Scatter the lime zest and the remaining ginger-garlic mixture over the lobsters. In a small measuring jar, stir together the lime juice and the remaining 1 cup/240 ml coconut milk and pour around the lobsters. Drizzle all with the sherry and sesame oil.

Cover the baking dish with heavy-duty aluminum foil and transfer to the oven. Steam in the oven until the lobster meat is firm and opaque throughout and the rice is tender and creamy, about 2 hours.

CONTINUED

Arrange a lobster half on each of four plates. Discard the chiles and stir the cilantro into the coconut milk in the pan; spoon some sauce over each lobster. Pass the remaining pan sauce at the table for dipping.

WORKING WITH LIVE LOBSTERS

Shellfish like crabs, lobsters, oysters, mussels, and clams all must be used live in the kitchen, because they decompose quickly after death. Adding them to hot water is accepted by many as a humane way to cook (and kill) shellfish, and one a good share of people who eat shellfish are comfortable with undertaking at home. In other instances, such as grilling or broiling lobster halves or as in this slow-steaming recipe, the cook is required to split the live animal and arrange it for cooking, possibly presenting a different comfort level for the home chef. But a sure hand and a swift cut with a well-sharpened knife makes the task equally humane, and opens a wide variety of dramatic and delicious ways to serve this special seafood.

To split a live lobster, put the lobster on a cutting board set in a rimmed baking sheet. Uncurl the tail and lay it out flat. Insert the tip of a sharp chef's knife into the back of the lobster, right at the seam where the head and body shells meet, with the edge of the blade facing the tail. In one motion, bring the knife down the centerline of the body, splitting the whole lobster in half. Now turn the lobster over and make the same cut on the under side to finish breaking the shell cleanly in two. The lobster will separate into two halves.

Place the two halves cut-side up on your cutting board. Remove the sand sack from the head and discard. Remove the light green tomalley from the carapace and, if present, the long sack of dark green roe that runs down the back of the lobster. These can be saved and used to flavor or thicken a sauce or as a garnish. The lobster is now ready for stuffing.

SALMON
⟡ OVEN-STEAMED ⟡
OVER ONIONS AND GARLIC

Farmed salmon is rich fish, different from its wild brethren. It is both milder in flavor and way richer in fat, which melts elegantly through the fish's flesh during long slow steaming. In this recipe, the salmon is steamed with citrus to complement its richness and imbedded with an aromatic composed butter, flavored exotically with cardamom and thyme.

PREP TIME: 15 minutes	**COOKING TIME:** about 4 hours	**STORE:** Best served immediately.	*Makes* **6** *servings*

» 1 tbsp olive oil

» 2 medium yellow onions, halved and thinly sliced

» 5 garlic cloves, finely chopped

» Coarse sea salt and freshly ground black pepper

» ½ lemon, thinly sliced

» ½ lime, thinly sliced

» ½ orange, thinly sliced

» 2 tbsp unsalted butter, room temperature

» 2 tsp ground cardamom

» 2 tsp dried thyme

» ½ tsp fine sea salt

» 2 lb/910 g farmed salmon fillet, in 1 large piece, pin bones and skin removed (see Skinning a Fish Fillet box, page 59)

Preheat the oven to 200°F/95°C.

Drizzle the bottom of a baking dish with ½ tbsp of the olive oil. Add the onions and spread in an even layer. Scatter the garlic over the onions and season with coarse sea salt and pepper. Arrange the citrus slices in an even layer on top of the onions and garlic, drizzle with the remaining ½ tbsp olive oil, and set aside.

In a small bowl, beat together the butter, cardamom, thyme, and fine sea salt until thoroughly blended.

Cut diagonal slits into the flesh of the salmon and fill each slit with a little of the seasoned butter mixture. Put the salmon, slit-side up, on top of the citrus slices. Cover the baking dish with heavy-duty aluminum foil and put in the oven. Steam in the oven until the flesh flakes to gentle pressure, about 4 hours.

Carve the fish carefully into six portions and arrange a portion on each of six plates, with some of the onion mixture as a bed for the fish or scooped alongside. Serve immediately.

VARIATION: IN A SLOW COOKER
Set up the onions, garlic, and citrus in the bottom of a 6-qt/5.7-l slow cooker. Prepare the salmon fillet as directed and lay it on top of the onions. Cover and cook on low for 3 hours.

SLOW-STEAMED
❧ SEA BASS ❧
WITH CINNAMON AND CHAI

In my Omar Khayyam alter ego, I have a fantasy of paneling a small room in my hut with cinnamon bark, where I will sip chai tea and slurp curry. I suspect this recipe may be the first step in the realization of that little haven. In this slow-steaming preparation, a whole fish rests on bits of cinnamon bark and is cooked over a pot of barely simmering chai tea. The vapors rising from the chai are so subtle and diffuse, it takes a good hour for the fish to cook through—so long that its flesh can't help but absorb a healthy dose of spiced perfume.

Note that this recipe calls for a large steaming basket, bamboo or metal, with a lid.

PREP TIME: 10 minutes	COOKING TIME: about 1 hour	STORE: Best served immediately.	Makes **2** TO **3** servings

- » 1 chai tea bag
- » 2 cups/480 ml boiling water
- » One whole sea bass, about 2 lb/ 910 g, cleaned, scaled, and fins trimmed by the fishmonger
- » 1 tbsp Homemade Curry Seasoning (page 83) or good-quality store-bought curry powder, such as Chef Salt Bamboo Curry
- » 2 tsp toasted sesame oil
- » 3 cinnamon sticks, broken with a hammer into long shards
- » 1 tbsp hoisin sauce
- » 1 tsp fresh lemon juice
- » 2 green onions, white and tender green parts, thinly sliced

Steep the tea bag in the boiling water for 5 minutes. Discard the tea bag.

Make three or four diagonal slits through the skin and deeply into the flesh of the fish on both sides. Rub the skin, the meat inside the slits, and the body cavity of the fish with the curry powder; drizzle all over with the sesame oil.

Pour the tea into a saucepan big enough to fit your steamer basket nested in the top. Put the saucepan over low heat and the steaming basket on top of the saucepan. Scatter the cinnamon shards over the bottom of the basket and put the fish on the bed of cinnamon. Cover the basket and steam very gently (the tea should barely bubble) for 1 hour until the flesh flakes to gentle pressure. Check the tea in the bottom of the steamer halfway through to make sure it is not boiling dry. Add ¼ cup/60 ml more water if you think the tea level is too low.

While the fish is steaming, mix the hoisin sauce and lemon juice in a small bowl; set aside.

When the fish is done, remove the basket from the pot. Mix ¼ cup/60 ml of the steaming tea liquid into the hoisin mixture.

Lift the fish with some of the cinnamon onto a serving platter. Drizzle with sauce and scatter the green onions over all. Serve immediately.

CHAPTER 5

· SLOW ·

GRILLING

For most of us, grilling means a hot fire, a thick steak, and quick cooking. But there's a whole other way to grill. It's low and slow and practically foolproof. Also known as indirect grilling, it involves moderate heat concentrated on one side of the grill and a large area away from the fire for cooking. You need to keep the lid down or the food won't cook because most of the heat will escape, like trying to bake a cake with the oven door open. You'll also let out all that wonderful smoke from the coals.

To set up a gas grill for indirect grilling, light some burners but leave the others off. For a two-burner gas grill, light just one side and put the food over the other, unheated side. If your grill has three or more burners, you can light one side of burners or light the outside burners and put the food over the unheated middle area.

On a charcoal grill, the principle is the same: set up the grill to create an unheated area for cooking and a heated area for the coals. For the most even cooking, rake the coals to opposite sides of the grill and leave the center unheated. However, if your grill is small, you'll get a larger cooking area by raking the coals to one side of the grill. You'll need to replenish the coals about once an hour.

As with all types of live fire grilling, once a fire is set the temperature is maintained by opening or closing vents in the base and/or lid of the grill. For low to medium temperatures, the vents should be about halfway open (see chart on facing page).

For fatty meats like pork shoulder, beef brisket, and skin-on duck, you'll need to put a disposable aluminum drip pan beneath the food. A drip pan not only prevents flare-ups but also acts like a roasting pan, catching flavorful juices than can be turned into a sauce when the food is done cooking.

❧ SLOW-GRILLING TEMPERATURES ❧

HEAT	TEMPERATURE	COAL APPEARANCE	COAL BED THICKNESS	GRATE HEIGHT	VENTS	COUNTING BY THOUSANDS *
Medium	300°F–350°F/ 150°C–180°C	Medium ash; visible glow	3 in/7.5 cm; split bed	4 in/ 10 cm	70% open	8 times
Medium-low	250°F–300°F/ 120°C–150°C	Medium-thick ash; faint glow	2 in/5 cm; split bed	5 in/ 12 cm	60% open	10 times
Low	200°F–250°F/ 95°C–120°C	Thick ash; spotty faint glow	1½ in/4 cm; split bed	5 in/ 12 cm	50% open	11 times

* At this temperature, you should be able to hold your hand, palm down, about 4 in/10 cm above the grill grate for the count ("1 one thousand, 2 one thousand . . .") listed in the chart without having to withdraw your hand.

BBQ'D YAMS

WITH ROOT BEER MOLASSES

Tubers like potatoes and yams are perfect candidates for slow cooking directly in hot coals. It is important to allow the coals to burn down before burying the spuds to ensure that they heat up gradually. Here the finished potatoes are slathered with a tangy sweet butter flavored with sassafras and molasses.

PREP TIME: 15 minutes	**COOKING TIME:** about 1 hour	**STORE:** Best eaten within a few hours.	*Makes* **4** TO **6** *servings*

» 4 orange-fleshed sweet potatoes, 12 to 16 oz/340 to 455 g each, scrubbed

» 2 tbsp dark rum

» 1 cup/240 ml root beer

» ¼ cup/60 ml molasses

» 1 tbsp cider vinegar

» 3 tbsp unsalted butter

» Sea salt and freshly ground black pepper

Build a fire in a charcoal grill or campfire grill and let burn into a hot coal bed at least 2 in/5 cm deep. Leave the grill grate off so the coals are accessible. Let the coals burn down until they are thickly coated with ash.

Prick each sweet potato several times with a fork, then bury them directly in the coals, raking the coals to nearly cover the potatoes. Cook until a skewer slides in and out of the center easily, about 1 hour, turning once or twice.

While the sweet potatoes are cooking, in a saucepan over medium-high heat, combine the rum, root beer, molasses, and vinegar. Bring to a boil and cook until reduced to one-fourth of the volume, about 10 minutes. Remove from the heat and let cool for 5 minutes. Stir in the butter until melted and season to taste with salt and black pepper; set aside.

Using tongs, lift the sweet potatoes from the coals. Brush off any loose ash and put on a platter or plates. Let cool a few minutes, then cut each sweet potato in half lengthwise and mash the flesh of each half with a fork. Drizzle on the root beer–molasses sauce and serve.

HONEY-BARBECUED
STUFFED SQUASH

In some ways, hard-skinned vegetables are a lot like tough meats: they are often full of flavor when cooked, but need plenty of time to take on flavor and succulence. This makes them perfect candidates for a smoky sojourn on a grill. In this recipe, a sweet and tangy barbecue sauce is slathered over the hard interior of a butternut squash. As the flesh of the squash softens, it is permeated with the flavors of the sauce.

PREP TIME: 15 minutes	COOKING TIME: about 1½ hours	STORE: for up to 3 days, covered in the refrigerator. Reheat gently in a low oven.	Makes 4 servings

- » 1 butternut squash, about 2 lb/ 960 g, quartered lengthwise and seeded
- » 4 tbsp/55 g unsalted butter, melted
- » 4 tbsp/60 ml honey
- » 1 tbsp ketchup
- » 1 tbsp apple cider vinegar
- » ½ tsp sea salt
- » ⅛ tsp freshly ground black pepper
- » Vegetable oil for greasing

Light a grill for indirect medium heat, about 300°F/150°C. If using a charcoal grill, build a small charcoal fire at one end of the grill. If using a gas grill, set a burner at one end of the grill to medium-low.

Prick the flesh of the squash with a fork in a few spots without going all the way down to the skin. Whisk together the melted butter, honey, ketchup, vinegar, salt, and pepper in a small bowl. Brush the honey all over the cut sides and cavities of the squash.

Brush the grill grate with oil. Put the squash on the grill away from the heat over a drip pan filled with ½ in/12 mm hot water. Cover the grill and cook until the squash is tender (a fork should slide in and out of the flesh easily), about 1 hour 20 minutes. Instruct guests to scoop the squash from the skin when serving.

SLOW-GRILLED

CHICKEN

Maybe you don't actually like your grilled chicken black and crusty; you just don't know how to make it any other way. All that's about to change. This foolproof grilled chicken can't burn because it never gets close to a flame, and yet because it stays near a fire for several hours, it has plenty of time to take on a charcoal flavor and burnished golden crust.

MARINATING TIME: 6 to 12 hours PREP TIME: 15 minutes	COOKING TIME: 2 to 3 hours	STORE: for up to 3 days, covered in the refrigerator. Reheat gently in a low oven.	*Makes* **4** *servings*

» **1 whole frying chicken, 3 to 4 lb/1.4 to 1.8 kg, split in half lengthwise**

» ½ cup Mojito Mop (page 147)

» ¼ cup dark rum

» ¼ cup/60 ml olive oil

» **Coarse sea salt and freshly ground black pepper**

Put the chicken halves in a large zippered plastic bag. Add the mop and rum, squeeze out the excess air, seal the bag, and refrigerate for at least 6 hours and up to 12 hours.

Light a grill for indirect low heat, about 200°F/95°C. If using a charcoal grill, build a small charcoal fire at one end of the grill. If using a gas grill, set a burner at one end of the grill to medium-low. Put the grill grate on the grill and clean the grill grate with a wire brush.

Remove the chicken halves from the marinade and pat dry. (Discard the marinade.) Coat the chicken with the olive oil and season with salt and pepper. Put the chicken halves on the grill away from the fire, angling the pieces so that the legs face the coals and the breasts face away. Cover the grill, and grill until the juices in the thickest part of one of the thighs run clear when the skin is pierced, or an instant-read thermometer inserted into the thickest part of a thigh (but not touching bone) registers 160°F/70°C, 2 to 3 hours. If using charcoal, you will need to replenish the coals once or twice during cooking. Serve immediately.

APPLE-BRINED
⟿ FRESH HAM ⟾

A whole fresh ham, cut from the top or bottom round of a pork thigh, is a substantial roast. Leaner than a pork shoulder with bigger, more intact muscles, and richer than a pork loin, which tends to dry out during grilling, a fresh ham is regal. This one is seasoned with a classic paprika-based barbecue rub and doused repeatedly during grilling with herb-infused apple cider spiked with bourbon.

BRINING TIME: 12 to 24 hours **PREP TIME: 30 minutes** **SEASONING TIME: 1 hour**	**COOKING TIME: 7 to 9 hours**	**STORE: for up to 3 days, covered in the refrigerator. Reheat gently in a low oven.**	*Makes* **12 TO 14** *servings*

FOR THE BRINE:

» 2 tbsp coarse sea salt
» 2 tbsp poultry seasoning
» 4 cups/960 ml apple cider
» 1 cup/240 ml bourbon

» 1 boneless whole fresh ham (uncured), inside or outside round, 8 to 10 lb/3.6 to 4.5 kg, rolled and tied by the butcher
» Vegetable oil for rubbing

FOR THE RUB:

» 1 tbsp paprika
» 1 tbsp coarse sea salt
» 2 tsp freshly ground black pepper
» 2 tsp cayenne pepper
» 2 tsp garlic powder
» 2 tsp onion powder
» 2 tsp rubbed sage
» 1 tsp dried thyme
» 1 tsp sugar

To make the brine: Mix the ingredients in an extra-large (2-gal/7.5-l) zippered plastic bag.

Add the ham and close the bag. Shake and massage the brine into the meat, seal the bag, and refrigerate for at least 12 hours and up to 24 hours.

While the meat is brining, make the rub: In a small bowl, stir together all the ingredients. Set aside.

An hour before you are ready to light the grill, remove the meat from the brine and pat dry. Reserve the brine. Rub all over with the spice mixture and set aside at room temperature for about 1 hour. Coat the meat with oil. While the meat is seasoning, bring the brine to a boil over medium-high heat and boil for a full 3 minutes. Remove from the heat and let cool to room temperature.

Light a grill for indirect low heat, about 200°F/95°C. If using a charcoal grill, build a small charcoal fire at one end of the grill. If using a gas grill, set a burner at one end of the grill to medium-low. Put the grill grate on the grill and clean the grill grate with a wire brush. Set a small pan of water on the grill grate to one side, near the coals.

Put the ham, fatty-side up, on the grill away from the heat. Cover the grill and cook until the meat is browned and cooked to medium-well (about 160°F/70°C on an instant-read thermometer), 7 to 9 hours.

136 Cooking Slow

After 1½ hours of cooking, put the ham in a disposable aluminum pan and begin basting it with the boiled brine about every 30 minutes during the remaining cooking time. The pan helps to retain moisture in the meat and keep it from drying out. If your grill has a temperature gauge, it should stay around 200°F/95°C during the entire cooking time. If using charcoal, refresh the coals about once an hour during cooking.

When the ham is done, transfer to a cutting board, tent loosely with aluminum foil, and rest for 10 minutes. Carve on the diagonal against the grain into thin slices and serve immediately.

PORK CHOPS

Pork is naturally low in moisture. In the past, it was kept juicy by lots of fat running through the meat; but much modern pork has been engineered to be as lean as chicken breast, so if you want pork moist you have to hold on to the wee bit of moisture that it has. Brining helps by upping the juiciness by as much as 10 percent; but even more important is adopting slow cooking for many cuts.

Lean pork begins to dry out when it reaches an internal temperature of about 150°F/65°C. If it is being grilled over a 500°F/260°C fire, the exterior parts of the chop will dry before the interior is up to temperature. Keeping the grill near 150°F/65°C is ideal, but difficult to maintain. I have found that 200°F/95°C is a good compromise, allowing enough heat to produce smoke but not so much that the chops cook too fast.

MARINATING TIME: 4 to 12 hours PREP TIME: 15 minutes SEASONING TIME: 1 hour	COOKING TIME: about 3 hours	STORE: for up to 3 days, covered in the refrigerator. Reheat gently in a low oven.	*Makes* **4** *servings*

» 2 cups/480 ml beer, any type

» 2 tbsp smoked salt such as red alder– or hickory-smoked (see Smoked Salt and Pepper box, following)

» 2 tbsp granulated sugar

» 4 thick bone-in pork rib chops, each about 12 oz/340 g and at least 1 in/2.5 cm thick

» 2 tbsp smoked paprika

» 2 tsp brown sugar

» 2 tsp ancho chili powder

» 1 tsp freshly ground black pepper

» Vegetable oil for rubbing

Mix the beer, smoked salt, and granulated sugar in a large zippered plastic bag. Add the pork chops, squeeze out any excess air, and seal the bag tightly. Refrigerate for at least 4 hours and up to 12 hours.

While the chops are brining, stir together the smoked paprika, brown sugar, chili powder, and black pepper in a small bowl; set aside.

About 1 hour before you are ready to light the grill, put 3 large handfuls of hardwood chips in a disposable aluminum pan and add water to cover; set aside. Remove the meat from the brine and pat dry. (Discard the brine.) Rub with the smoked paprika mixture and set aside at room temperature for about 1 hour. Coat the meat liberally with oil.

Light a grill for indirect low heat, about 200°F/95°C. If using a charcoal grill, build a small charcoal fire at one end of the grill. If using a gas grill, set a burner at one end of the grill to medium-low. Drain the water from the soaking chips and put the pan holding the chips directly on the low fire. Put the grill grate on the grill and clean the grill grate with a wire brush. Set a small pan of water on the grill grate to one side, near the coals.

CONTINUED

Put the chops on the grill away from the heat, cover the grill, and cook until the meat is nicely browned and cooked to medium (about 150°F/66°C on an instant-read thermometer), about 3 hours. If your grill has a temperature gauge, it should stay around 200°F/95°C during the entire cooking time. If using charcoal, refresh the coals about once an hour during cooking. You can add more soaked wood chips if you want an extra-smoky flavor.

SMOKED SALT AND PEPPER

One of the simplest ways of getting natural smoked flavors into recipes is by seasoning with smoked salt. Although cheap smoked salts can be made with artificial flavoring, naturally smoked salts are far more aromatic and delicious. They range from mild (try guava wood–smoked salt from Hawaii) to campfire-pungent (red alder wood–smoked salt from the Pacific Northwest). You can purchase high-quality smoked salts in most high-end groceries or gourmet shops or from numerous sources online.

Smoked black pepper is an equally good way to get authentic natural smoke flavor into any recipe, although not as commonly available. It would be fun to seek it out and explore the culinary possibilities of the combined smokiness and spiciness.

❧ LAMB SHANKS ❧

Ideal for braises and the slow-baking techniques in this book, which use long slow heat to tenderize the shank meat and melt the fat and marrow, applying shanks to the dry heat of the grill requires finagling. The answer lies in a long marinating time. This recipe calls for tenderizing the lamb in buttermilk for at least half a day. Some of the marinade is reserved for mopping, which ensures the lamb gets the moisture it needs.

MARINATING TIME: 12 to 24 hours **PREP TIME: 15 minutes, plus 1 hour to rest meat**	**COOKING TIME: about 3 hours**	**STORE: for up to 3 days, covered in the refrigerator. Reheat gently in a low oven.**	*Makes* **4** *servings*

» 6 tbsp/90 ml olive oil, plus more for greasing

» 2 cups/480 ml buttermilk

» 4 garlic cloves, minced

» 4 tsp coarse sea salt

» 1 tsp freshly ground black pepper

» ½ tsp cayenne pepper

» 1 tbsp sugar

» 1 tbsp chopped fresh oregano

» 4 lamb shanks, about 12 oz/ 340 g each

» ¼ cup/60 ml fresh lemon juice

» ¼ cup/10 g chopped fresh flat-leaf parsley

In a bowl, whisk together 3 tbsp of the olive oil, the buttermilk, garlic, salt, black pepper, cayenne, sugar, and oregano. Pour half of the marinade into a large zippered plastic bag and add the lamb shanks. Squeeze out the excess air, seal the bag, and refrigerate for at least 12 hours and up to 24 hours. Refrigerate the remaining marinade in a closed container.

About 1 hour before you are ready to light the grill, remove the meat from the marinade and pat dry. Set aside at room temperature for about 1 hour. Rub the meat with the remaining 3 tbsp olive oil.

Stir the lemon juice and parsley into the reserved marinade; set aside.

Light a grill for indirect low heat, about 200°F/95°C. If using a charcoal grill, build a small charcoal fire at one end of the grill. If using a gas grill, set a burner at one end of the grill to medium-low. Put the grill grate on the grill and clean the grill grate with a wire brush. Set a small pan of water on the grill grate to one side, near the coals.

Brush the grill grate with oil. Put the lamb shanks on the grill away from the heat, cover the grill, and cook until an instant-read thermometer inserted into the thickest part of a shank (but not touching bone) registers 175°F/80°C, about 3 hours. Turn and baste with the reserved parsley marinade until the shanks are shiny and moistened on all sides, 4 to 6 times. Remove from the grill, let rest briefly (see Resting Slow-Cooked Meats box, page 33), and serve.

COFFEE

⟳ BBQ BRISKET ⟲

This recipe is not for a spontaneous afternoon or quick after-work grill time; but what you sacrifice in speed, you reap in extreme tenderness and a buildup of flavor that permeates every morsel of meat.

The trick is keeping the fire far away from the food. If you have a barrel grill, build a small fire at the far end of the grill and place the brisket at the opposite end. In a kettle grill, spread the hot coals in an arc along one edge of the fire box and put the meat in the open area as far away from the coals as you can. In a gas grill, set a burner at one end on low and put the meat at the other end. The cooking may be slow, but the actual work occupies minutes rather than hours.

CHILLING TIME: 8 to 24 hours **PREP TIME:** 30 minutes, plus 1 hour to rest meat	**COOKING TIME:** 6 to 8 hours	**STORE:** for up to 3 days, covered in the refrigerator. Reheat gently in a low oven.	*Makes* **8** TO **10** *servings*

FOR THE RUB:

» 3 tbsp unsweetened cocoa powder
» 1 tbsp ancho chili powder
» 1 tbsp coarse sea salt
» 1 tbsp dark brown sugar
» 1 tsp ground cinnamon
» 1 tsp chipotle chili powder
» ½ tsp ground aniseed
» ½ tsp garlic powder
» ½ tsp onion powder
» ½ tsp freshly ground black pepper
» 1 tsp dried oregano, preferably Mexican
» Pinch of dried cloves

FOR THE MOP:

» Juice of 2 lemons
» 2 cups/480 ml brewed coffee
» ¼ cup/60 ml molasses
» 2 tbsp balsamic vinegar
» 2 tsp coarse sea salt

» 1 flat or center-cut beef brisket, 4 to 5 lb/1.8 to 2.3 kg, trimmed, with ¼ in/6 mm of fat on one side
» Vegetable oil for rubbing

To make the rub: Mix the cocoa powder, ancho chili powder, salt, brown sugar, cinnamon, chipotle chili powder, aniseed, garlic powder, onion powder, pepper, oregano, and cloves in a small bowl.

To make the mop: Mix the lemon juice, coffee, molasses, vinegar, and salt in a separate bowl. Mix 1 tbsp of the rub into the mop. Set aside.

Rub the remaining rub all over the brisket. Cover tightly in plastic wrap and refrigerate for at least 8 hours and up to 24 hours.

About 1 hour before you're going to grill, remove the meat from the refrigerator to bring to room temperature. Rub the meat liberally with oil. Light a grill for indirect low heat, about 200°F/95°C. If using a charcoal grill, build a small charcoal fire at one end of the grill. If using a gas grill, set a burner at one end of the grill to medium-low. Clean the grill grate with a wire brush.

Put the brisket, fatty-side up, on the grill away from the heat, cover the grill, and cook until the brisket is deeply browned and blackened in spots and cooked to well-done (about 170°F/77°C on an instant-read thermometer), 6 to 8 hours.

CONTINUED

FOR THE SAUCE:

» **1 cup/240 ml brewed coffee**
» **1 cup/240 ml ketchup**
» **¼ cup/60 ml dark mustard**
» **⅓ cup/75 ml honey**
» **2 tbsp apple cider vinegar**
» **2 tsp coarse sea salt**
» **2 tsp freshly ground black pepper**
» **2 tbsp hot-pepper sauce**

During the entire cooking time, brush the surface of the brisket on both sides liberally with the mop whenever the surface looks dry, about every 30 minutes. After 1½ hours of cooking, put the brisket in an aluminum foil pan and return the pan to the grill away from the heat; cover the grill and continue cooking. The pan helps to retain moisture in the brisket and keep it from drying out. Once the brisket is in the pan, you need to mop only the top, or fatty, side. If your grill has a temperature gauge, it should stay around 200°F/95°C during the entire cooking time. If using charcoal, refresh the coals about once an hour during cooking. You can add chunks of wood (such as hickory, mesquite, or apple) to the fire periodically if you want a smoky flavor.

Anytime during grilling, make the sauce: In a small saucepan, whisk together the coffee, ketchup, mustard, honey, vinegar, salt, black pepper, and hot sauce. Bring to a boil over medium heat and simmer until slightly thickened, about 4 minutes. Remove from the heat and let cool to room temperature.

When the brisket is done, trim off any excess fat (not too much, though; the crispy bits taste great) and carve across the grain on the diagonal into thin slices. Serve with the sauce.

VARIATION: IN A SLOW COOKER

Rub, refrigerate, and rest the brisket as directed in the recipe. Built a hot fire in a charcoal grill or preheat a gas grill to high. Brown the brisket well on both sides, about 10 minutes per side. Put the browned meat in a 6-qt/5.7-l slow cooker. Prepare ½ recipe of mop and pour over the brisket. Cover and cook on low until the brisket is fork-tender, about 8 hours. Prepare the sauce and serve as directed.

BBQ TRI-TIP

Tri-tip, a relatively small (1½ to 2½ lb/680 g to 1.2 kg) curved, triangular muscle cut from the bottom of the sirloin just above the leg, is just about the tastiest cut of beef that you can buy at a reasonable price. Unfortunately, it is not universally available. Developed in the late 1950s by a butcher in Santa Maria, California, who chose to rotisserie-roast the cut rather than grind it for hamburger, the popularity of tri-tip spread quickly throughout the central coast of California. It can still be hard to find tri-tip anywhere but on the West Coast, since most meat packers send all of their tri-tip to California. If you can't find one, you can substitute a similar-size boneless bottom sirloin roast.

In this recipe, I took the traditional barbecue elements of a rub, a mop, and a sauce and gave them a multinational Asian flavor palate—five-spice powder in the rub, rice wine vinegar in the mop, and hoisin for the sauce.

CHILLING TIME: 4 to 24 hours **PREP TIME: 20 minutes, plus** **1 hour to rest meat**	**COOKING TIME: about 3 hours**	**STORE: for up to 3 days, covered** **in the refrigerator. Reheat** **gently in a low oven.**	*Makes* **4 TO 6** *servings*

» 3 tbsp five-spice powder

» 2 tbsp coarse sea salt

» 2 tsp freshly ground black pepper

FOR THE MOP:

» 1 cup/240 ml fresh orange juice

» 3 tbsp honey

» 3 tbsp rice wine vinegar

» 1 tri-tip roast, 2 to 2½ lb/910 g to 1.2 kg

» Vegetable oil for rubbing

FOR THE SAUCE:

» ¼ cup/60 ml hoisin sauce

» 2 tsp peeled and minced fresh ginger

» 3 garlic cloves, minced

» 2 tbsp rice wine vinegar

» 2 tbsp soy sauce

» 1 tsp hot-pepper sauce

In a small bowl, stir together the five-spice powder, salt, and black pepper.

To make the mop: Mix the orange juice, honey, and rice vinegar in a separate bowl. Mix 1 tbsp of the spice mixture into the mop. Set aside.

Rub the remaining spice mixture all over the tri-tip. Cover tightly in plastic wrap and refrigerate for at least 4 hours and up to 24 hours.

About 1 hour before you're going to grill, remove the meat from the refrigerator to bring to room temperature. Rub the meat liberally with oil. Light a grill for indirect low heat, about 200°F/95°C. If using a charcoal grill, build a small charcoal fire at one end of the grill. If using a gas grill, set a burner at one end of the grill to medium-low. Clean the grill grate with a wire brush.

Put the meat, fatty-side up, on the grill away from the heat, cover the grill, and cook until the meat is nicely browned and cooked to medium (about 135°F/57°C on an instant-read thermometer), about 3 hours.

CONTINUED

During the entire cooking time, brush the surface of the meat on both sides liberally with mop whenever the surface looks dry, about every 30 minutes. If your grill has a temperature gauge, it should stay around 200°F/95°C during the entire cooking time. If using charcoal, refresh the coals about once an hour during cooking. You can add chunks of wood (like hickory, cherry, or apple) to the fire periodically if you want a smoky flavor.

Anytime during grilling, make the sauce: In a small saucepan, stir together the hoisin, ginger, garlic, vinegar, and soy sauce. Bring to a boil over medium heat and stir in the hot-pepper sauce. Remove from the heat and let cool to room temperature.

Carve the tri-tip across the grain on the diagonal into thin slices. Serve with the sauce.

VARIATION: IN A SLOW COOKER

Rub, refrigerate, and rest the meat as directed in the recipe. Build a hot fire in a charcoal grill or preheat a gas grill to high. Brown the tri-tip well on both sides, about 10 minutes per side. Put the browned meat in a 6-qt/5.7-l slow cooker. Prepare ½ recipe of the mop and pour over the meat. Cover and cook on low until the tri-tip is fork-tender, about 6 hours. Prepare the sauce and serve as directed.

MOJITO FISH STEAKS

Fish steaks are often preferred over fillets for grilling because they are sturdier and don't tear if they happen to stick to a grill grate. This all-purpose recipe is designed to go with any fish steak. Although it is possible to cook fish steaks quickly, slowing the process down a bit yields exceptionally moist and tender results, The connective tissue in the fish just starts to soften as the protein in the flesh sets, yielding a creamy, evenly cooked fish, with very little drying.

PREP TIME: 30 minutes	COOKING TIME: about 1 hour	STORE: for up to 2 days, covered in the refrigerator. Reheat gently in a low oven.	Makes **4** servings

» 4 firm-fleshed fish steaks such as salmon, swordfish, kingfish, or sable, each 6 to 8 oz/170 to 225 g and about ¾ in/2 cm thick

» 2 tbsp olive oil, plus more for brushing

» Sea salt and freshly ground black pepper

FOR THE MOJITO MOP:

» 3 tbsp light rum

» Juice and finely grated zest of 1 large lime

» 1 tbsp canola oil

» 1 tsp hot-pepper sauce

» 1 tbsp sugar

» 4 tbsp/10 g chopped fresh mint leaves

Light a grill for indirect low heat, about 200°F/95°C. If using a charcoal grill, build a small charcoal fire at one end of the grill. If using a gas grill, set a burner at one end of the grill to medium-low. Put the grill grate on the grill and clean the grill grate with a wire brush.

Coat the fish steaks with the 2 tbsp olive oil and season with salt and pepper. Set aside for 5 minutes.

Meanwhile, make the mop: In a small bowl, stir together the rum, lime juice, canola oil, hot-pepper sauce, sugar, and 3 tbsp of the mint leaves.

Brush the grill grate with olive oil. Put the fish on the grill away from the heat, spoon 1 tbsp of the mop over each fish steak, cover the grill, and cook until the fish steaks flake to gentle pressure, about 1 hour, basting with the mop about every 5 minutes.

Serve each fish steak scattered with the remaining chopped mint and the lime zest.

SMOKED GOUDA CHEESECAKE

This fabulous grilled hors d'oeuvre cheesecake is alive with savory flavors: apple wood–smoked ham, single-malt Scotch, smoked salt, smoked cheese, and sautéed onion. The cake bakes slowly over a very low, smoky fire. By allowing the batter to set slowly, the cake gets ample time, about 4 hours, to absorb great smoky flavor while the low, slow baking makes for an ultimately creamy cake from edge to edge. Chill the cake thoroughly before serving with sliced bread or crackers. It will keep in the refrigerator, tightly wrapped, for a week or more, and can be frozen for up to 2 months.

PREP TIME: 1 hour	COOKING TIME: about 4 hours	STORE: for up to 8 days, covered, in the refrigerator.	*Makes* **24** *servings*

- » 2 tbsp unsalted butter
- » 1 medium yellow onion, finely chopped
- » 1 garlic clove, minced
- » 8 oz/225 g smoked ham, preferably apple wood–smoked, finely chopped
- » 1½ lb/680 g cream cheese, at room temperature
- » ¼ cup/60 ml whiskey, preferably a smoky, peaty Scotch such as Laphroaig
- » 3 tbsp red wine vinegar
- » 2 tsp smoked salt such as red alder– or hickory-smoked (see Smoked Salt and Pepper box, page 140)
- » 1 tsp freshly ground black pepper, preferably smoked
- » 1 tsp smoked paprika
- » 5 eggs, large or extra-large
- » 8 oz/225 g smoked Gouda cheese, shredded
- » ⅓ cup/45 g grated Parmesan cheese, plus more for dusting
- » Vegetable oil spray
- » 2 tbsp dried bread crumbs
- » Sliced black bread for serving

Put 3 large handfuls of hardwood chips in a disposable aluminum pan, add water to cover, and soak for 1 hour.

Light a grill for indirect low heat, about 200°F/95°C. If using a charcoal grill, build a small charcoal fire at one end of the grill. If using a gas grill, set a burner at one end of the grill to medium-low.

Melt the butter in a large skillet over medium-high heat. Add the onion and sauté until lightly browned, about 7 minutes. Add the garlic and stir until aromatic, about 30 seconds. Remove from the heat and stir in the ham; set aside.

In a large bowl, using an electric mixer set on medium-high, beat the cream cheese until fluffy. Beat in the whiskey, vinegar, salt, black pepper, and paprika until smooth. Add the eggs and beat just long enough to incorporate, scraping down the sides of the bowl with a spatula as needed to keep the mixture smooth. Scrape the onion and ham mixture from the skillet into the batter. Add the Gouda and Parmesan and stir just until the batter is well blended and smooth; do not overmix.

Coat a 2-qt/2-l soufflé dish with vegetable oil spray and dust the inside with Parmesan and the bread crumbs. Scrape the batter into the prepared dish.

Drain the wood chips and put the pan holding the chips directly on the low fire. Put the grill grate on the grill and clean the grill grate with a wire brush. Set the cheesecake on the grill grate away from the fire.

Cover and grill until the cake is set and a tester inserted in the center comes out with a small bit of moist-set cheesecake batter clinging to it, about 4 hours. Replenish the wood chips and coals, if using charcoal, every hour.

Let cool to room temperature in the pan, unmold, and chill before serving. Serve with black bread slices.

CHAPTER 6

—

· SLOW ·

FRYING

When I was a kitchen rookie, I learned that frying must always be done at temperatures above 375°F/190°C or the food would absorb frying oil and become sodden with grease. I'm here to tell you: I was duped. Cooking in oil at temperatures as low as 170°F/75°C produces fish and meat of unprecedented lushness—soft and moist throughout, and so pervasively scented with whatever spices or herbs are added to the recipe that one would swear the meat was crossbred with seasoning.

The technique is not really so novel. It has several classic culinary predecessors: confit and *poêle*. The first is a traditional method of producing fatty meats, like duck, goose, and pork by simmering the flesh in an abundance of the animal's fat. After the meat is cooked and cooled, a layer of fat solidifies on top, sealing the perishable meat in an oxygen- and bacteria-free state. As long as the meat and fat remain cold enough to keep the fat solid (not difficult in a root cellar during the winter), the cooked meat will stay fresh.

Poêle is more esoteric. It is a technique of poaching meat, most commonly small game, in fat. Because wild game is leaner than farm-raised meat, it benefits from added fat during cooking. This is why it is typically layered with fatback or bacon for roasting, or mixed with fat into paté or sausages.

The added benefit of simmering ingredients in barely warmed oil is the resulting oil itself. Leftover oil that has been used for poaching a chicken with garlic or salmon with herbs is heady stuff, wonderful in a salad dressing, for sautéing, or for drizzling over coldcuts.

 POTATOES

Many of us have been taught that frying is fatty business: especially if the fat is not hot enough, the food will absorb oil and end up unappealing or even unhealthful. Better wisdom about the science of frying has come to save us. For the vast majority of the frying time, water is being flushed from the food, and as long as water is flowing out, oil can not flow in.

This holds true even for slow frying. And by slowing everything down, the potatoes remain fluffy and slightly moist in the center while they get nice and crispy around the edges. Be patient and don't raise the heat too fast, so the crust becomes super-thick and crunchy but never gets darker than gold. This one takes some attention, but the stellar results are well worth the effort.

PREP TIME: 10 minutes	COOKING TIME: about 1¼ hours	STORE: Best served immediately.	Makes **4** servings

» 2 tbsp unsalted butter or lard

» 1½ lb/680 g red-skinned potatoes, scrubbed and cut in ½-in/12-mm dice

» 2 pinches of fine sea salt

» 1 or 2 grindings of black pepper

» Small handful of coarsely chopped fresh flat-leaf parsley

Put a cast-iron skillet over medium-low heat. Add the butter and melt until the fat is covered with bubbles and begins to hiss around the edges. This will take about 5 minutes. Resist the temptation to raise the heat.

Distribute the potatoes over the bottom of the pan. Sprinkle with the salt. Cover and cook until they just start to become tender, about 20 minutes. Uncover and use the spatula to free the potatoes from the pan bottom. Invert the "potato pancake," using your other hand to help stabilize the potatoes on the spatula. It's okay if the potatoes break apart, but try to keep them in as few large pieces as you can manage.

Raise the heat a *little* (barely to medium) and cook, uncovered, until the edges start to get crisp, about 30 minutes, turning every 10 minutes (3 turns in all).

Raise the heat a little more (to medium). Cook until very brown and crisp, about 20 more minutes, turning every 5 minutes (four turns in all). If your potatoes are very moist, it may take a few minutes longer and need another turn or two. What you want is a creamy, moist interior and a surface that is brown and crunchy, not just superficially crispy.

Just before the potatoes are done, sprinkle with the pepper and parsley. Serve and eat immediately.

SOFT-SCRAMBLED
EGGS
WITH CHÈVRE

Does anyone really need a recipe for scrambled eggs? Maybe not; but then you encounter that rare specimen, the perfect scrambled egg, a mound of rich yellow curds, creamy, glistening, and plump, and you find yourself wondering, "How?"

Temperature has a profound effect on the texture of eggs. The lower the heat, the slower and more evenly the eggs will set. Slow-scrambled eggs have creamy, moist, custard-like consistency throughout. Here the impact is heightened by a last-minute addition of tangy, creamy goat cheese.

PREP TIME: 5 minutes	**COOKING TIME:** about 20 minutes	**STORE:** Serve immediately. (This dish will not last!)	Makes **4** servings

» 8 large eggs

» 3 tbsp milk or heavy (whipping) cream

» ½ tsp fine sea salt

» ¼ tsp freshly ground black pepper

» 1 tbsp unsalted butter

» 2 oz/55 g fresh chèvre

Crack the eggs into a bowl. Beat with a large fork or whisk until well combined. Add the milk, salt, and pepper and continue beating until foamy.

In a nonstick skillet over low heat, melt the butter. Slant the pan to coat the bottom evenly with butter.

Add the beaten eggs to the pan and wait until you can see a few soft curds form along the bottom of the pan. This will take 2 to 3 minutes. Using a sturdy plastic spatula, gently scrape the egg from the bottom of the pan. Keep scraping slowly until a moist, soft custard forms. This will take about 15 minutes.

Crumble the chèvre into the egg and keep scraping and turning the soft mound of custardy egg until it is set to the degree of doneness you want. Immediately scrape onto a plate and serve.

CHICKEN LEG
AND LEMON CONFIT

This modern-day confit is enlivened with salted lemons. The salt concentrates the lemon flavors, which helps to flavor both the chicken and the oil during cooking. The leftover oil is spectacular for frying potatoes.

The confit can be kept submerged in its oil in the refrigerator for up to 1 month; rewarm gently over low heat. The olive oil floating in the dish can be used for roasting vegetables (especially potatoes or beets), drizzled over blanched green beans, or used to sauté boneless chicken breast, pork chops, or veal scallops.

CHILLING TIME: 12 to 24 hours **PREP TIME:** 10 minutes	**COOKING TIME:** about 12 hours	**STORE:** submerged in its oil in the refrigerator, tightly covered, for up to 1 month. Rewarm gently over low heat.	*Makes* **8** *servings*

» 8 chicken legs

» 2 tbsp coarse sea salt

» 2 lemons, preferably organic, scrubbed, halved, seeded, and coarsely chopped

» 10 garlic cloves, smashed

» 2 tsp cracked black peppercorns

» 1 tsp saffron

» 6 cups/1.4 l olive oil

» 12 pitted Kalamata olives, halved

Put the chicken in a bowl and rub with 1 tbsp of the salt. In another bowl, toss the lemons with the remaining 1 tbsp salt. Layer the chicken in a glass or ceramic bowl or dish with the garlic cloves and refrigerate for at least 12 hours or up to 24 hours; leave the lemons out at room temperature for the same amount of time.

Preheat the oven to 200°F/95°C. Remove the chicken from the refrigerator. Pick out the garlic cloves and reserve. Rinse off excess salt from the chicken and pat dry. Arrange half of the chicken legs in a Dutch oven in a single layer. Scatter half the garlic, chopped lemons, peppercorns, and saffron over top. Pour in 3 cups/720 ml of the olive oil. Repeat to make a second layer with the remaining chicken, garlic, lemons, peppercorns, saffron, and olive oil. Push the chicken down so that it is submerged in the oil. Cover the pot, transfer to the oven, and cook until the meat from the chicken loosens from the bone, about 12 hours.

Lift the chicken from the oil along with some of the lemons, pepper, garlic, and saffron. Scatter the olives over the top and serve.

YOUNG CHICKEN POÊLE

WITH BABY STEWING VEGETABLES

Poêle, **a way of poaching** delicate ingredients in fat or oil, is akin to the more well-known method called *confit.* The main difference is the amount of fat. A confit is cooked in enough fat to cover all of the ingredients by at least 1 in/2.5 cm. Its principal purpose is preservation, but in the process creates meats and vegetables that are meltingly tender, enriched by the flavor-infused fat. *Poêle* calls for less fat—just enough to generously coat—but yields the same lush results: falling-apart-tender meat, rich aromas, and a luxurious mouthfeel. Although any bird can be cooked in this method, it is particularly advantageous to use small, young birds (see Young Chicken box, following). They are more easily surrounded by the oil and they more readily absorb the fragrance of vegetables and spices poaching along with them.

PREP TIME: 10 minutes	**COOKING TIME:** 5 to 6 hours	**STORE:** for up to 3 days, covered in the refrigerator. Rewarm gently in a low oven.	*Makes* **4** *servings*

» **1 young chicken, 3 to 4 lb/1.4 to 1.8 kg, quartered**

» **Coarse sea salt and freshly ground black pepper**

» **6 tbsp/90 ml olive oil**

» **12 small new carrots, trimmed and scrubbed**

» **8 small new potatoes, scrubbed and halved**

» **16 thawed frozen pearl onions**

» **½ tsp dried thyme**

» **½ tsp dried rosemary, crushed**

» **2 garlic cloves, minced**

» **¾ cup/115 g frozen peas, thawed**

» **2 tsp chopped fresh tarragon**

Preheat the oven to 175°F/80°C.

Season the chicken quarters all over with a liberal sprinkling of salt and pepper. Heat 2 tbsp of the olive oil in a Dutch oven over medium heat. Sear the skin side of the chicken quarters until lightly browned, about 5 minutes; transfer to a plate and set aside.

Add the carrots, potatoes, and pearl onions and sauté until lightly browned, about 5 minutes. Season with the thyme, rosemary, garlic, and salt and pepper.

Put the chicken quarters on top of the vegetables and drizzle the remaining 4 tbsp olive oil over all. Cover the Dutch oven and put in the middle of the oven; cook until the chicken meat is ready to fall from the bone, 5 to 6 hours.

CONTINUED

To serve, transfer the chicken pieces to a platter. Stir the peas and tarragon into the other vegetables, and spoon around the chicken. Spoon the juices remaining in the bottom of the cooker over top.

VARIATION: IN A SLOW COOKER

Follow the recipe, using a large heavy skillet to brown the chicken and vegetables instead of a Dutch oven, if you prefer. Pour and scrape the cooked vegetables into the slow cooker and put the chicken pieces on top. Drizzle with the remaining oil, cover, and cook on low for 5 to 6 hours. Finish as described.

YOUNG CHICKEN

At one time "young chicken," meaning a bird about 1 month old, was a springtime specialty (hence, of course, the phrase "spring chicken"), but nowadays almost all chickens are barely older than 35 days. Those sold specifically as "young" tend to be free-range rather than cage raised, and more carefully fed and processed. Young hens are called pullets, and are sometimes sold under that name. A young chicken should be relatively small (no more than 4 lb/1.8 kg), with pale skin and a sternum bone that is completely flexible.

SLOW-FRIED
PORK LOIN
IN MUSTARD OIL

Roasting pork loin is hit or miss; a few minutes too long can be the difference between juicy and dry. But not anymore. By immersing the loin in an oil bath, in this case flavored with mustard seed, the pork is protected from drying out. Strain and save the delicious oil in the refrigerator for making salad dressings or mayonnaise, or for sautéing meat. Serve with Slow-Fried Potatoes (page 153).

CHILLING TIME: 8 to 12 hours **PREP TIME:** 10 minutes	**COOKING TIME:** about 2 hours, plus 10 minutes for heating frying oil	**STORE:** for up to 5 days, covered in the refrigerator. Reheat gently in a low oven.	*Makes* **6** *servings*

» **1 pork loin, about 3 lb/1.4 kg, trimmed of fat and silver skin**

» **1 tbsp coarse sea salt**

» **1 tsp freshly ground black pepper**

» **4 cups/960 ml canola oil**

» **1 cup/130 g brown mustard seed**

Rub the pork with the salt and pepper. Set on a rack on a baking sheet and refrigerate for at least 12 hours and up to 24 hours.

Preheat the oven to 175°F/80°C.

Combine the oil and mustard seed in a Dutch oven and place over medium heat until the oil reaches 350°F/177°C on a deep-frying thermometer. A wooden chopstick or the end of a wooden spoon inserted into the oil will emit bubbles when the oil is at the right temperature.

While the oil is heating, remove the pork from the refrigerator. Pat dry. When the oil is up to temperature, turn off the heat. Using tongs, carefully submerge the meat in the hot oil. Cover the pot, transfer to the oven, and cook until the pork is 150°F/66°C, about 2 hours.

Lift the pork from the oil onto a baking sheet to catch any oil drips. Carve the pork across the grain on the diagonal into thin slices. Drizzle with some of the mustard-scented oil and serve.

SCAMPI
"BOILED" IN OIL

Scampi are small lobsters native to the waters surrounding Europe. In Italy, the word is used to describe large shrimp, the cooked meat of which resembles true scampi. Because of this Italian connection, scampi has come to mean any preparation for shrimp or crayfish that is flavored with garlic, and that is true here; a whole head goes into the flavorful poaching oil with the shrimp.

The slow-cooking temperature in this recipe is so low, the shrimp simply warm to doneness and stay there. Don't be afraid of the amount of oil; the shrimp absorb flavor and emerge extra moist but not greasy. This is a supremely easy and elegant dish for entertaining. Serve the scampi dressed with lemon and herbs or use them to flavor a risotto or pasta dish. Save the leftover oil in the refrigerator for making salad dressings, mayonnaise, or for sautéing fish or seafood.

CHILLING TIME: 3 to 12 hours **PREP TIME:** 10 minutes	**COOKING TIME:** about 1 hour plus 10 minutes to heat frying oil	**STORE:** for up to 2 days, covered in the refrigerator. Bring to room temperature before serving.	*Makes* **6** *servings*

- » 2 lb/910 g jumbo shrimp, peeled and deveined
- » 1 tbsp coarse sea salt
- » 3 cups/720 ml olive oil
- » 1 head garlic, peeled and coarsely chopped
- » Juice of 1 lemon
- » ¼ cup/10 g chopped fresh flat-leaf parsley

Toss the shrimp with the salt on a rimmed sheet pan. Refrigerate, uncovered, for at least 3 hours and up to 12 hours. It is important to keep the shrimp uncovered. The salt will draw moisture to the surface of the shrimp and you want that to evaporate, encouraging the development of a crisp crust during frying. Don't worry about making the fridge smell fishy; the salt will keep odors at bay.

Preheat the oven to 175°F/80°C. Put the olive oil in a large, oven-proof saucepan or skillet and place over medium heat until the oil reaches 300°F/149°C on a deep-frying thermometer.

Remove the shrimp from the refrigerator and pat dry. Toss with the garlic.

When the oil is up to temperature, turn off the heat. Add the shrimp, cover, and transfer to the oven. Poach the shrimp until opaque throughout and firm to the touch, about 1 hour.

Transfer the shrimp and garlic from the hot oil with a slotted spoon to a serving bowl. Toss with the lemon juice and parsley and serve immediately.

SALMON

POACHED IN HERBED OLIVE OIL

I have been accused of hyperbole, but here I must objectively report that this recipe will change your life. There are countless quick salmon recipes done under a broiler, on a grill, or in a hot oven, and though they may mostly be delicious and easy, none can come close to the silken consistency and complete ease of slow-cooking this regal fish. It is almost impossible to overcook, and the flesh is rendered custard-soft and succulently moist. Save the leftover oil in the refrigerator and use for salad dressings, mayonnaise, or sautéing fish.

CHILLING TIME: 6 to 12 hours **PREP TIME:** 10 minutes	**COOKING TIME:** 3 to 5 hours	**STORE:** for up to 2 days, covered in the refrigerator. Bring to room temperature before serving.	*Makes* **6** *servings*

- » 2 lb/910 g salmon fillet
- » 1 tbsp coarse sea salt
- » 6 cups/1.4 l olive oil
- » Leaves from 24 fresh herb sprigs such as rosemary, dill, tarragon, thyme, flat-leaf parsley, and/or mint, in any combination (about 1½ cups/60 g)
- » Juice of 1 lemon

Rub the flesh side of the salmon fillet with the salt. Wrap in plastic and refrigerate for at least 6 hours and up to 12 hours.

Preheat the oven to 175°F/80°C. Put the olive oil in a fish poacher or Dutch oven and put over medium heat until the oil reaches 350°F/177°C on a deep-frying thermometer. A wooden chopstick or the end of a wooden spoon inserted into the oil will emit bubbles when the oil is at the right temperature.

While the oil is heating, remove the salmon from the refrigerator. If using a fish poacher, brush the rack with a thin film of oil. If using a Dutch oven, fold a long sheet of heavy-duty foil in half lengthwise and brush with a thin film of oil. Scatter a small handful of herbs on the rack or foil, and put the fish on it skin-side down. Scatter the remaining herbs on the flesh side of the fish and press lightly to help them adhere.

When the oil is up to temperature, turn off the heat. Submerge the fish on its rack or foil strip into the pot of oil. If you are using foil, the ends of the strip will hang over the sides of the Dutch oven. Cover the pot, transfer to the oven, and poach until the fish is firm to the touch, 3 to 5 hours. The oven temperature is low enough that you do not have to worry about overcooking.

Lift the fish from the oil onto a sheet pan to catch any oil drips, using the rack or foil sling for support. Slide the fish from the rack onto a serving platter and spoon some of the warm oil over the top. Drizzle with the lemon juice and serve.

CHAPTER 7

· SLOW ·

COOKER

Slow cooking is an ancient mode of making food, nearly as old as home cooking itself. Simmering a pot of meat and vegetables by the side of a fire while one was out building a homestead was what "home cooking" originally meant. But with the development of the Crock-Pot, slow cooking was divorced from the fireside and became electric, streamlined, and convenient. Now with the dawn of home sous vide machines, slow cooking has evolved again, taking on the mantle of modernist cuisine. Both contemporary slow-cooking appliances warm ingredients gently, blending flavors and softening tough meats like the fireside cauldron, but that's where the connection ends.

The differences have to do with moisture. Slow cookers and sous vide cookers promote less evaporation than other methods of slow cooking, and for that reason slow cooker and sous vide recipes require far less liquid than cooking in any other way—about 2 tbsp/30 ml of liquid ingredients per person for sauces, ¼ cup/60 ml for stews, and ½ cup/120 ml for soups, or about one-fourth of what one would use for simmering on a stove top.

But reduced evaporation does not just pose a challenge for calculating the amount of sauce in a finished recipe; it has a significant impact on the finished flavor. The problem is water. Water makes food moist but it also dilutes flavor. In traditional forms of cooking—roasting, baking, sautéing, frying—water loss concentrates flavorful components in the ingredients, making their flavors fuller and deeper. In a slow cooker, water evaporates, but it gets trapped on the inside of the lid and drips back into the cooker, resulting in food that can end up tasting watery and bland.

CURRIED
VEGETABLES

Curries are complex, interweaving dozens of spices into a heady stew. The work isn't hard, but it does take time for all of the flavors to meet and marry—a natural for the slow cooker. You do need to sauté the spices ahead of time to release their aroma, but once that's completed, the slow cooker does all of the work for you.

PREP TIME: 30 minutes	**COOKING TIME:** 4 to 5 hours on high, 7 to 8 hours on low	**STORE:** for up to 3 days, covered in refrigerator. Reheat gently in a low oven or over low heat.	*Makes* **8** *servings*

» 2 leeks, white and tender green parts thoroughly washed

» 2 lb/910 g mixed vegetables, such as rutabaga, carrots, parsnips, and celery

» 2 tbsp olive oil

» 2 tbsp minced fresh ginger

» 4 garlic cloves, minced

» 1 tbsp fresh thyme leaves

» 1 tsp ground turmeric

» 2 tsp ground coriander

» 1 tsp ground cumin

» 1 tsp sea salt

» ½ tsp freshly ground black pepper

» One 28-oz/800-g can diced tomatoes, with juice

» One 15-oz/430-g can chickpeas, drained and rinsed

» 1 large butternut squash, about 2 lb/910 g

» 1 cinnamon stick

» 1 tbsp honey

» 1 tbsp fresh lemon juice

» 1 to 2 tsp hot-pepper sauce

» 2 tbsp chopped fresh cilantro

Peel and prepare the leeks, rutabaga, carrots, parsnips, and celery as necessary, and cut into ½-in/12-mm chunks. Heat the oil in a large deep skillet over medium-high heat. Add the cut vegetables and sauté until the carrots are barely tender. Add the ginger, garlic, thyme, turmeric, coriander, cumin, salt, and black pepper and stir to disperse; cook for 1 minute. Add the tomatoes with their juices and the chickpeas and heat to boiling; set aside.

Meanwhile, peel, seed, and cut the butternut squash into 2-in/ 5-cm chunks. Put the squash in a 6-qt/5.7-l slow cooker. Pour the contents of the skillet over the top and tuck the cinnamon stick into the sauce. Cover and cook for 4 to 5 hours on high or 7 to 8 hours on low.

While the curry cooks, in a bowl, stir together the honey, lemon juice, and hot-pepper sauce. When the curry is done, remove the cinnamon stick, drizzle the honey mixture over top, and toss gently to disperse. Scatter the cilantro over the top and serve.

BAKED BEANS

Baked beans are usually cooked with meat—traditionally smoked, fatty pork meat—to lend them richness and the redolence of a campfire. But I love this delicious vegetarian rendition, just as full of picnic spirit, and allowing the flexibility for serving any diners a good dose of protein in their comfort food. Replacing the ham hock with roasted bell peppers preserves the expected smokiness and adds a dimension of tang and fruit that cuts through the inherent blandness of the beans. Although you could bake these beans in an oven (see Slow-Simmered Bourbon-Bacon Beans, page 100), the slow cooker does a better job of preserving moisture, which is a boon when you can't rely on lovely bits of melting pork fat to add succulence.

| PREP TIME: 15 minutes (including roasting the peppers), plus 1 hour to overnight (depending on how you soak the beans) | COOKING TIME: 10 to 12 hours | STORE: for up to 5 days, covered in the refrigerator. Reheat gently in a low oven or over low heat. | Makes **8** servings, with leftovers |

- » 1 lb/455 g dried white beans such as navy beans or pea beans
- » 2 tsp vegetable oil
- » 1 medium yellow onion, cut into ½-in/12-mm dice
- » 2 roasted red bell peppers (see Roasting Bell Peppers box, facing page), seeded and cut into ¼-in/6-mm dice
- » 4 cups/960 ml good-quality low-sodium vegetable broth
- » 1 cup/225 g ketchup
- » ½ tsp hot chili powder

Pick over the beans for stones or grit. Rinse in a colander and drain well. Put the beans in a bowl and add water to cover by at least 3 in/7.5 cm. Let soak overnight, then drain. Alternatively, put the beans in a saucepan, add water to cover by at least 3 in/7.5 cm, and bring to a boil. Boil for 3 minutes, then remove from the heat and let the beans soak for 1 hour. Drain and put the beans in the slow cooker.

Heat the oil in a large heavy skillet over medium-high heat. Add the onion and sauté until barely tender, about 3 minutes. Add the roasted bell peppers and the broth and bring to a boil. Remove from heat and stir in the ketchup; pour and scrape into the slow cooker, mix to coat the beans, and cook on low for 10 to 12 hours, until the beans are tender and the sauce is lightly thickened.

Stir in the chili powder and cook for 10 minutes to allow the flavors to blend. Serve.

ROASTING BELL PEPPERS

Working with one bell pepper at a time, place it directly on the grate of a gas burner set on high; or put several peppers directly on the rack under a broiler set to the highest setting or on the grill rack over a hot fire. As the skin on one side of the pepper burns, turn to another side. Repeat until the skin is uniformly burnt all over. Be careful to keep the pepper moving so that the flesh under the skin doesn't char. Transfer the roasted peppers to a paper bag or a bowl, close the bag or cover the bowl, and set aside until cool. When the pepper is cool enough to handle, peel off the burnt skin with your fingers. Remove the stems and seeds before preparing as directed in a recipe.

BBQ PORK
AND BEANS

Canned pork and beans have become so commonplace in our pantries, most of us have forgotten how easy, and delicious, and cheap it is to mix up a cauldron of the stuff from scratch. Although I usually use canned beans for slow cooker recipes, starting with dried makes a difference in this case. Because canned beans are precooked, they get mushy before they get a chance to absorb all of the flavors of the sauce. And since the difference between succulence and mush takes no more work, it's well worth the extra time in the cooker.

PREP TIME: 25 minutes, plus 1 hour to overnight (depending on how you soak the beans)	**COOKING TIME:** 8 to 10 hours	**STORE:** for up to 5 days, covered in the refrigerator. Reheat in a low oven or over low heat.	*Makes* **8** *servings*

» 1 lb/455 g dried white beans such as navy beans, pea beans, or cannellini

» 1 lb/455 g boneless pork shoulder, trimmed of fat and cut into 1-in/2.5-cm cubes

» 3 tsp Southwest-Style Spice Rub (facing page)

» 8 oz/225 g pork belly, finely diced

» 1 medium yellow onion, cut into ½-in/12-mm dice

» 2 carrots, peeled and cut into ½-in/12-mm dice

» 1 celery stalk, cut into ½-in/12-mm slices

» 1 tsp ground cumin

» 1 tbsp all-purpose flour

» 3 cups/720 ml Old Chicken Broth (page 91)

» ½ cup/120 ml All-Purpose Barbecue Sauce (facing page) or your favorite store-bought or homemade barbecue sauce

» One 14½-oz/415-g can diced tomatoes, drained

Pick over the beans for stones or grit. Rinse in a colander and drain well. Put the beans in a bowl and add water to cover by at least 3 in/7.5 cm. Let soak overnight, then drain. Alternatively, put the beans in a saucepan, add water to cover by at least 3 in/7.5 cm, and bring to a boil. Boil for 3 minutes, then remove from the heat and let the beans soak for 1 hour. Drain.

Rub the pork cubes with 2 tsp of the spice rub; set aside.

Cook the pork belly in a large deep skillet, preferably cast-iron, over medium heat until the bottom of the pan is coated with a generous layer of fat. Remove the cooked pork belly and reserve. Turn the heat up to medium-high and brown the pork cubes in the fat; transfer to a 6-qt/5.7 l slow cooker. Add the soaked and drained beans and the pork belly, and toss to combine.

Add the onion, carrots, and celery to the skillet and sauté until tender and lightly browned, about 3 minutes, stirring often. Stir in the cumin, the remaining 1 tsp of spice rub, and the flour and stir to coat the vegetables. Add the broth and simmer until lightly thickened, stirring often. Stir in the barbecue sauce and tomatoes and pour into the slow cooker. Stir to combine, cover, and cook for 8 to 10 hours on low, until the beans are tender. Stir and serve.

Southwest-Style Spice Rub

This is a homemade version of a spice blend I produce and sell, Chef Salt Bacon BBQ. It's not nearly as smoky, but easy to mix up.

Makes about ½ cup/80 g

» **1 tbsp fine sea salt**
» **2 tbsp paprika**
» **¼ cup firmly packed light brown sugar**
» **1 tsp ancho chili powder**
» **1 tsp chipotle chili powder**
» **½ tsp ground cumin**
» **½ tsp ground black pepper**

Mix together the salt, paprika, brown sugar, ancho chili powder, chipotle chili powder, cumin, and pepper until well blended. Store in a tightly sealed container in a dark cabinet for up to 1 month.

All-Purpose Barbecue Sauce

There is no reason to spend the money on commercially produced barbecue sauce when you've got one that is this delicious and easy to throw together.

Makes about 1 cup/240 ml

» **⅓ cup/75 ml ketchup**
» **3 tbsp spicy brown mustard**
» **3 tbsp apple cider vinegar**
» **3 tbsp light brown sugar**
» **1 tbsp Tabasco or other hot-pepper sauce**
» **½ tsp freshly ground black pepper**

In a bowl, stir together the ketchup, mustard, apple cider vinegar, brown sugar, Tabasco, and pepper until well blended. Store in the refrigerator in a tightly closed container for up to 2 weeks.

CHESAPEAKE BAY
PULLED PORK

Pulled pork is identified closely with the Carolinas (vinegar-basted in North Carolina; mustard south of the border), where the barbecue tradition calls for dousing juicy shreds of roasted pig in a mop and piling it ecstatically on a soft bakery bun. In this recipe, I turn the tables by rubbing a pork shoulder with aromatic Old Bay Seasoning, and move the geography north a state or two. Although barbecue is the traditional method for pulled pork, I find a slow cooker does a better job. Using the barbecue takes time and attention, basting constantly with mop, and even if you are vigilant, the meat has a tendency to crust over and dry out. Trapping all of the juices in a slow cooker eliminates all the hassle and gives you foolproof succulence.

SEASONING TIME: 1 hour at room temperature or overnight in the refrigerator **PREP TIME:** 15 minutes	**COOKING TIME:** 8 to 10 hours	**STORE:** for up to 5 days, covered in the refrigerator. Reheat gently in a low oven or over low heat.	*Makes* **6** *servings*

» **1 tbsp onion powder**

» **1 tbsp garlic powder**

» **1 tbsp sweet paprika**

» **2 tbsp Old Bay Seasoning**

» **1 tbsp light brown sugar**

» **3 lb/1.4 kg boneless pork shoulder (picnic ham) or boneless country-style pork ribs**

» **2 tbsp vegetable oil**

» **2 garlic cloves, minced**

» **¾ cup/180 ml Old Chicken Broth (page 91)**

» **6 large soft rolls, such as hamburger buns (optional)**

» **1½ cups/285 g coleslaw (optional)**

In a bowl, stir together the onion powder, garlic powder, paprika, Old Bay, and brown sugar. Remove 1 tbsp of the spice mix and reserve; rub the remainder all over the pork. Wrap the pork in plastic wrap and set aside for 1 hour or refrigerate overnight, whichever is more convenient.

Heat the oil in a large skillet over medium high heat. Add the pork and sear until nicely browned on all sides. Transfer to a 4-qt/3.5-l slow cooker. Add the garlic to the skillet, and cook for 10 seconds. Add the broth and the reserved spice mixture, and bring to a boil, scraping any browned bits from the bottom of the pan into the liquid. Pour over the pork, cover, and cook for 8 to 10 hours on low, until the pork is fork-tender.

Remove the pork from the cooker, cut into slices ½ in/12 mm thick, and shred the slices into bite-size pieces with two forks. Return the pork to the cooker and toss to coat with the sauce. Serve immediately, or keep warm for up to several hours. Serve on soft rolls with coleslaw, if desired.

BEEF STEW

WITH RED WINE AND ROSEMARY

This bistro-style beef stew is nearly effortless. The wine does all the work. Even though you don't want to use a sweet wine for beef stew, be careful that your wine is not too dry. Tannins, the astringent chemicals that give wines a drying effect on the tongue, indicate good potential for a wine's longevity, but they tend to turn bitter in cooking, especially when simmered for many hours in a slow cooker. Serve with lots of crusty bread, if desired, for mopping up the gravy.

PREP TIME: 20 minutes	COOKING TIME: 6 to 8 hours	STORE: for up to 3 days, covered in the refrigerator. Reheat gently in a low oven or over low heat.	*Makes* **6** *servings*

» ½ cup/60 g flour

» 2 tsp coarse sea salt

» ½ tsp ground black pepper

» 3 lb/1.4 kg trimmed beef chuck, cut into 1½-in/4-cm cubes

» 3 tbsp olive oil

» 3 strips bacon, cut into ½-in/12-mm pieces

» 2 medium onions, cut into ½-in/12-mm dice

» 2 medium turnips, peeled and cut in ½-in/12-mm dice

» 3 medium carrots, peeled and sliced ½-in/12-mm thick

» 2 celery ribs, sliced ½-in/12-mm thick

» Pinch of ground cloves

» 1½ cup/360 ml full-bodied red wine, such as Cabernet Sauvignon

» 1 cup/240 ml vegetable cocktail juice, such as V8

» 8 fresh rosemary sprigs

» 2 bay leaves

» 2 tbsp chopped fresh flat-leaf parsley

Combine the flour, salt, and pepper in a mixing bowl. Add the beef cubes and toss to coat evenly with flour; pat off the excess flour and reserve.

Heat 1 tbsp of the olive oil in a large deep skillet over medium-high heat. Brown the beef in two or three batches, adding more oil with each batch, as needed. As the beef is browned, transfer to the slow cooker.

Reduce the heat to medium, add the bacon, and cook until crisp. Add the onions, turnips, carrots, and celery, and sauté until browned, about 5 minutes. Add the reserved seasoned flour and stir until browned, about 3 minutes. Add the ground cloves and wine and heat to boiling. Add the vegetable juice and return to a boil; pour over the beef in the slow cooker.

Tie the rosemary sprigs and bay leaves in a small bundle with kitchen twine and bury in the center of the cooker. Cover and cook for 6 to 8 hours on low, until the beef and vegetables are fork-tender.

Remove the rosemary bundle. Stir in the parsley and serve.

CHOCOLATE
⤜ LAMB CHILI ⤛

Chili has a casual roadside reputation that belies its complexity. The dynamic mixture of peppers, spices, and herbs in homemade chili is as sensually complicated as the most sophisticated mole or cassoulet. In this recipe, I turn the tables on traditional cowboy chili by switching out beef for lamb. The results are slightly gamey and very rich. To underscore that richness, the chili is finished with chocolate, which smooths the sauce and moves the flavors in this hearty stew closer to those of a Mexican red mole. Serve with hot rice, or wedges of warm pita, if desired.

PREP TIME: 30 minutes	**COOKING TIME:** 4 to 5 hours on high, 8 to 9 hours on low	**STORE:** for up to 4 days, covered in the refrigerator. Reheat gently in a low oven or over low heat.	*Makes* **8** *servings*

- » 2 tbsp chili powder
- » 1 tbsp ground coriander
- » 2 tsp ground cumin
- » 1 tsp dried oregano
- » 1 tsp dried thyme
- » ½ tsp ground cardamom
- » 2 tbsp all-purpose flour
- » 3 lb/1.4 kg boneless leg of lamb, trimmed of fat and silver skin, cut into ½-in/12-mm pieces
- » Sea salt and freshly ground black pepper
- » 3 tbsp vegetable oil
- » 2 large yellow onions, diced
- » 1 medium eggplant, peeled and cut into ½-in/12-mm squares
- » 2 garlic clove, minced
- » 2 chipotle chiles en adobo, finely chopped, plus 1 tablespoon adobo sauce
- » 1½ cup/340 ml good-quality low-sodium beef broth
- » One 28-oz/794-g can diced tomatoes (not drained), preferably fire-roasted
- » Two 15½-oz/439-g cans white kidney beans, drained and rinsed
- » 2 oz/55g bittersweet chocolate (64% cocoa), finely chopped
- » 3 tbsp chopped cilantro

Mix the chili powder, coriander, cumin, oregano, thyme, cardamom, and flour in a small bowl; set aside.

Season the lamb with salt and pepper. Heat the oil in a large skillet over medium-high heat and brown the lamb in two batches, transferring each batch to a 6-qt/5.7-l slow cooker as it browns.

Add the onions and eggplant to the pan and sauté over medium-high heat until browned, about 4 minutes. Add the garlic and chipotle chiles and cook for about 30 seconds. Stir in the adobo sauce and the spice mixture, and sauté until aromatic, about 1 minute. Stir in the broth and tomatoes and stir until simmering and lightly thickened, about 5 minutes.

Pour the sauce into the cooker with the lamb. Cover and cook for 4 to 5 hours on high, or 8 to 9 hours on low, until the lamb is fork-tender. Stir in the beans and warm until heated through. Stir in the chopped chocolate and cilantro until the chocolate melts, about 1 minute before serving.

CLASSIC
CASSOULET

Cassoulet, the peasant-cum-gastronome casserole from Toulouse, is a time-honored gut-buster, and one of the most sophisticated dishes that is perfected by moving it from the oven to the slow cooker. Cooked in a slow cooker, cassoulet is effortless—it doesn't dry out, the flavors blossom beautifully, and all it takes at the end is a half hour in a medium-hot oven to crisp the topping.

PREP TIME: about 1 hour, plus overnight to soak the beans	COOKING TIME: 8½ to 10½ hours on low	STORE: for up to 5 days, covered in the refrigerator. Reheat gently in a low oven or over low heat.	*Makes* **12** *servings*

» 1 lb/455 g dried large white beans such as cannellini or baby limas

» 1 duck such as Muscovy or Pekin, about 4 lb/1.8 kg

» 1 lb/455 g boneless leg of lamb, cut into 2-in/5-cm cubes

» 2 tsp coarse sea salt

» ½ tsp freshly ground black pepper

» 8 oz/225 g garlic sausages, cut into 2-in/5-cm pieces

» 8 oz/255 g smoked sausages such as andouille, cut into 2-in/5-cm pieces

» 1 large yellow onion, chopped

» 2 large celery stalks, cut into ½-in/12-mm slices

» 4 garlic cloves, minced

» 1 tsp Homemade Italian Seasoning (page 90)

» ¼ tsp freshly grated nutmeg

» Pinch of ground cloves

» ½ cup/120 ml dry white wine

» 1 qt/960 ml good-quality low-sodium beef broth or chicken broth, or a mixture

» One 15-oz/430-g can diced tomatoes, drained

» ⅔ cup/75 g dried bread crumbs

» ¼ cup/10 g coarsely chopped fresh flat-leaf parsley

Pick over the beans for stones or grit. Rinse in a colander and drain well. Put the beans in a bowl and add water to cover by at least 3 in/7.5 cm. Let soak overnight, then drain.

Meanwhile, cut the duck into 8 serving pieces and trim off all visible fat and excess skin; reserve the duck pieces and duck fat and skin separately. Season the duck pieces and lamb with salt and pepper, and set aside.

Cook the duck fat and skin in a large heavy skillet over medium heat until between ¼ and ⅓ cup/60 and 75 ml fat is in the pan, about 4 minutes. Remove the solid pieces of fat and skin and discard. Brown the duck in the hot fat on both sides and set aside. Brown the lamb and set aside. Brown the sausage pieces on all sides, and set aside.

Add the onion and celery to the skillet and sauté until lightly browned. Add the garlic, Italian seasoning, nutmeg, and cloves and sauté until aromatic, about 1 minute. Add the wine and bring to a boil. Add the beef broth and tomatoes and bring to a boil.

To assemble the cassoulet, layer the beans and meats, in alternating layers (four of beans, three of meat), in a 6-qt/5.7-l slow cooker, starting and ending with beans. Pour the liquid over all. Cover and cook until the beans are tender, 8 to 10 hours on low.

Preheat the oven to 350°F/180°C/gas 4. Mix the bread crumbs and parsley in a small bowl and scatter over the top of the cassoulet. Bake until the top is browned and bubbling, about 30 minutes. Serve immediately.

DUCK-PORCINI
RAGOUT

Reminiscent of hunters' stew, this recipe plays up several magical combinations: the melding of dark duck meat with earthy mushrooms, and the marriage of opulent duck and fruity red wine. Rosemary and thyme add their herby perfume to the cooking liquid. You can ask your butcher or meat purveyor to cut up the bird, or use a very sharp knife to do it yourself. Serve with polenta or over buttered noodles, if desired.

PREP TIME: 20 minutes	**COOKING TIME:** 4 to 6 hours	**STORE:** for up to 3 days, covered in the refrigerator. Reheat gently in a low oven or over low heat.	*Makes* **4** TO **6** *servings*

» 4 to 5 lb/1.8 to 2.3 kg bone-in duck pieces, such as legs, thighs, and breast halves

» ¼ cup/30 g flour

» 1 tsp fine sea salt

» 1 tsp ground black pepper

» Pinch of ground cloves

» 1 large onion, cut into ½-in/12-mm dice

» 1 large carrot, peeled and cut into ½-in/12-mm dice

» 1 large celery rib, cut into ½-in/12-mm dice

» ½ lb/230 g assorted wild mushrooms, such as oyster, shiitake, or cremini, cut into ¼-in/6-mm slices

» 2 tsp chopped fresh rosemary

» 1 tsp fresh thyme leaves

» 1 cup/235 ml full-bodied red wine, such as Cabernet Sauvignon or Merlot

» ½ oz/14 g dried porcini mushrooms, rehydrated in 1 cup/235 ml hot beef broth, chicken stock, or water

» 1 cup/200 g canned diced tomatoes, drained

» 2 tbsp chopped fresh flat-leaf parsley

Remove the skin and visible fat from the duck pieces (see Poultry Skin box, facing page). Cut the breast pieces in half.

Heat a large deep skillet, preferably cast-iron, over medium heat. Add half of the duck skin and attached fat and cook until there is ¼ in/6 mm of melted duck fat in the pan, about 4 minutes. Remove the remaining skin and solid fat pieces and discard.

Comine the flour, salt, pepper, and cloves in a medium mixing bowl. Add the duck pieces and toss to coat evenly with flour; pat off the excess flour and reserve.

Place the skillet containing the duck fat over medium-high heat. Brown the floured duck pieces on both sides, in batches. As the duck is browned, transfer to the slow cooker.

Reduce the heat to medium, add the onion, carrot, celery, and wild mushrooms to the pan and sauté until lightly browned, about 4 minutes. Add the reserved seasoned flour and stir until the vegetables are coated. Add the rosemary, thyme, and wine and bring to a boil. Add the soaked dried mushrooms and their soaking liquid and the tomatoes, bring to a simmer, and stir until the sauce is slightly thickened. Pour over the duck in the slow cooker and stir gently to coat.

Cover and cook for 4 to 6 hours on low, until the duck is very tender.

Garnish with the parsley and serve.

POULTRY SKIN

Poultry skin is full of flavor, luscious collagen, and calories. For dry-cooking methods, like roasting and baking, poultry skin crisps deliciously as it helps to protect the meat beneath and keep it moist. But when cooking poultry in liquid, the skin is a hindrance. It stays flabby and unpleasantly slimy and is best discarded. In this recipe, instead of adding oil for browning the duck and vegetables, you gently cook some of the duck skin in a dry skillet until its fat is rendered, becoming the only fat in the stew.

To remove the skin from duck or chicken pieces, simply peel it off like a tight stocking. If it doesn't remove easily, it is probably because there is a bit of membrane holding it in place. Slit the membrane with scissors or a small knife and keep peeling.

CHAPTER 8

—

· SOUS ·
VIDE

This chapter, like the one before, centers on slow-cooked dishes that are enhanced by machinery. These sous vide recipes are mostly written for ingredients that are too delicate to slow-cook by any other method—wild salmon, rack of lamb, filet mignon, soft-cooked eggs—whereas the slow cooker chapter concentrates on ingredients that are improved by hours of simmering, such as beans, root vegetables, and tough meats.

As I mentioned in the previous chapter, slow cookers promote less evaporation than other methods of slow cooking, requiring far less liquid, and resulting in concentrated flavors in your final dish. In sous vide cooking, because the ingredients are vacuum sealed, there is no possibility of evaporation. And prepare yourself for a textural revelation! Because the temperature regulation is extremely precise, you run no risk of overcooking your ingredients, resulting in tender, succulent, moist textures. Meats that go quickly from undercooked to overcooked, such as fish, are especially well-served by the sous vide method.

These recipes can be made in a SousVide Supreme (2.6 gl/10 l) or a SousVide Supreme Demi (2.3 gl/8.7 l), or using a thermal circulator–style sous vide, which clips on to any large pot.

WILD SALMON

WITH HORSERADISH, GINGER, AND DILL

Wild salmon is too lean for slow cooking in an oven or slow cooker. For those less precise methods, you need the fat content of a farmed salmon to protect the delicate flesh from drying out (see Salmon with Spiced Red Lentils and Bacon, page 57), but with sous vide the game plan shifts. Because you can set the cooking temperature to a super-low 125°F/51.6°C (not much hotter than hot tap water), you can serve perfectly moist wild fish and cook it untended for the better part of the day. In this recipe, I play off the assertive flavors of wild salmon with a piquant spicy-cool blend of horseradish and ginger.

PREP TIME: about 10 minutes	COOKING TIME: 1 to 4 hours	STORE: Store sealed fish raw for up to 3 days; does not store well after cooking.	Makes **4** servings

SPECIAL EQUIPMENT

» Vacuum sealer and 1 food-grade plastic cooking pouch, large enough to hold the salmon

» 1½ tbsp shredded fresh horseradish root
» 1 tbsp finely chopped fresh ginger
» 1 tbsp melted butter
» Juice of ½ lime
» 1½ lb/680 g wild salmon fillet, sockeye, coho, or king
» ½ tsp coarse sea salt
» ¼ tsp freshly ground black pepper
» 4 sprigs fresh dill

Combine the horseradish, ginger, butter, and lime juice in a small bowl. Season the flesh side of the salmon with the salt and pepper, then scatter the horseradish mixture over the fish. Arrange the fronds from the dill sprigs evenly over the fish.

Slip the salmon into a large cooking pouch. Seal the bag to 90 percent vacuum (dry setting on a FoodSaver machine). Refrigerate until you are ready to sous vide the fish.

Set the sous vide cooker to 125°F/51.6°C. If you are using a cooker with a circulator, close the rear pump flow switch and set the front switch to half open. When the water bath reaches temperature, add the vacuum bag and cook for at least 1 hour, but it will not overcook the fish to leave it in the water for up to 4 hours.

When the fish is done slow-cooking, remove the pouch from the water bath, snip open the sealed end, slip the fish onto a serving platter, and serve immediately.

SCOTCH BUTTER

SHORT RIBS

This is the third recipe for short ribs in this book. I have included it not because I am a short rib groupie, but because it highlights the meat's alter ego. Short rib recipes tend to be rich and stewy when braised in the style of a pot roast. And yet the cut of meat is a piece of rib roast, the same meat that we serve as prime rib.

By using the low and slow heat of sous vide, we can get fall-off-the-bone richness without cooking the meat past medium-rare. It takes a long time, 2 to 3 days, but the results are unlike any short rib you have ever had. The meat is infused deliciously with the honey-smoked fumes of Islay single-malt Scotch.

PREP TIME: about 10 minutes	COOKING TIME: 48 to 72 hours for sous vide; 12 minutes for browning	STORE: Store sealed browned meat for up to 1 week; store cooked sealed short ribs up to 2 days in refrigerator; rewarm in sealed pouch in simmering water.	*Makes* **4** *servings*

SPECIAL EQUIPMENT

» Vacuum sealer and 1 food-grade plastic cooking pouch, large enough to hold the ribs in a single layer

» 8 beef short ribs, about 4 to 5 in/10 to 12 cm long, about 8 oz/225 g each

» Coarse sea salt

» Cracked black peppercorns

» ¼ cup/55 g butter

» 1 cup/240 ml peaty single-malt Scotch, such as Laphroaig

» 1 cup/240 ml vegetable cocktail juice, such as V8

» 8 fresh thyme sprigs

Season the short ribs liberally with salt and pepper.

Melt the butter in a large skillet over medium-high heat until foaming. Add the short ribs and brown on all three of the meaty sides, about 1½ minutes per side. Do not crowd the pan; you might have to brown them in two batches. Remove to a large plate to cool.

Meanwhile, remove the pan from the heat and add the Scotch to the hot pan. Stir and scrape the bottom of the pan to integrate any flavorful brown bits. Reduce the heat to medium and bring to a boil. Add the vegetable juice and bring to a boil. Turn off the heat, and adjust seasoning with salt and pepper. Cool to room temperature.

Put the seasoned ribs into a large cooking pouch. Spoon the sauce over top and place a thyme sprig on each rib. Seal the bag to 85 percent vacuum (wet setting on a FoodSaver machine). Refrigerate until you are ready to sous vide the meat.

Set the sous vide cooker to 135°F/57.2°C. If you are using a cooker with a circulator, close the rear pump flow switch and set the front switch to fully open. When the water bath reaches temperature, add the vacuum bag and cook for 48 hours for firm but tender results, 72 hours for fall-off-the-bone results.

Remove the bag from the water bath, and snip open the sealed end. Pour the juices in the bag into a skillet and bring to a boil over medium-high heat. Slip the ribs onto a platter, and remove the thyme sprigs. When the sauce in the skillet has thickened to a glaze, about 2 minutes, pour over the ribs and serve.

FILET MIGNON
IN WILD MUSHROOM RAGÙ

Sous vide cookers allow you to regulate temperature to exact fractions of degrees, which means that more than any other cooking method, sous vide yields perfect doneness on meats. With tough cuts that are always cooked above well-done, this is not a big deal, but for pricey filet it makes all the difference in the world. In this effortless recipe, filet steaks are browned at the highest heat possible, to make a beautiful crust without cooking the interior, and heated in the sous vide to whatever degree of doneness you prefer. I have chosen medium-rare. While the steaks are cooking, an elegant wild mushroom sauce simmers, and when the two meet on a plate—pure opulence.

PREP TIME: about 15 minutes	**COOKING TIME:** 1 to 4 hours for sous vide; 15 minutes for cooking ragù	**STORE:** Store sealed browned steaks for up to 1 week; does not store well after cooking.	*Makes* **4** *servings*

SPECIAL EQUIPMENT

» **Vacuum sealer and 1 food-grade plastic cooking pouch, large enough to hold the steaks in a single layer**

» **Four 6-oz/170-g filet steaks or 1½ lb/680 g filet mignon roast, cut into 4 steaks**

» **Coarse sea salt and freshly ground black pepper**

» **4 tbsp/55 g unsalted butter**

» **½ oz/15 g dried wild mushrooms, finely chopped, any type**

» **¾ cup/180 ml hot water**

» **2 shallots, finely chopped**

» **8 oz/225 g mixed fresh mushrooms, such as oyster, shiitake, cremini, porcini, morels, or chanterelles, coarsely chopped**

» **½ cup/120 ml dry red wine**

» **¼ cup/60 ml tomato sauce**

» **2 cups/480 ml good quality low-sodium beef broth**

» **1 tbsp coarsely chopped fresh flat-leaf parsley**

Season the steaks with 1 tsp salt and ½ tsp pepper. Heat half of the butter in a large skillet, preferably cast-iron, over high heat until the butter starts to brown. Add the steaks and brown on all sides. The pan should be hot enough to brown each side in less than 1 minute. The steaks should remain as raw inside as possible.

Remove from the pan and turn off the heat. Put the browned steaks into a large cooking pouch, leaving space around each steak. Seal the bag to 90 percent vacuum (dry setting on a FoodSaver machine). Refrigerate until you are ready to sous vide the meat.

Set the sous vide cooker to 130°F/54.4°C. If you are using a cooker with a circulator, close the rear pump flow switch and set the front switch to fully open. When the water bath reaches temperature, add the vacuum bag and cook for at least 1 hour, but it will not overcook the steaks to leave them in the water for up to 4 hours.

While the steaks are slow-cooking, make the wild mushroom ragù. Combine the dried mushrooms and hot water in a small bowl and set aside for 10 minutes.

Add the remaining butter to the skillet and heat over medium-high heat until foamy. Add the shallots and the fresh mushrooms and sauté until the mushrooms brown a little, about 5 minutes.

Add the rehydrated mushrooms and their soaking liquid and the wine. Bring to a boil and boil for a full minute to evaporate excess alcohol. Stir in the tomato sauce and the beef broth and simmer until the sauce thickens slightly, about 5 minutes. Adjust the seasoning with salt and pepper; set aside.

When the steaks are done slow-cooking, remove the pouch from the water bath, snip open the sealed end, and slip the steaks onto a serving platter. Drain any juices that have collected around the steaks into the mushroom ragù.

Heat the ragù to a simmer over medium-high heat. Stir in the parsley and spoon over the steaks. Serve immediately.

RACK OF LAMB

WITH MUSTARD MINT CRUST

Cooking a rack of lamb in a pot of warm water is surreal, but when you taste the results, perfectly medium-rare from end to end, meltingly tender, you may never roast a rack of lamb again. Like all sous vide recipes, the doneness temperature is precise and the rack can't overcook, making this an ideal method for entertaining. All it needs for finishing is a coating of seasoned bread crumbs and less than 10 minutes in a hot oven to brown.

PREP TIME: about 20 minutes	**COOKING TIME:** 1 to 4 hours for sous vide; 8 minutes for browning	**STORE:** Store sealed racks raw for up to 2 weeks; does not store well after cooking.	*Makes* **4** *servings*

SPECIAL EQUIPMENT

» Vacuum sealer and 2 food-grade plastic cooking pouches

» 2 Frenched racks of lamb, 1¼ lb/570 g each, 8 ribs each

» 1 tsp coarse sea salt

» ½ tsp freshly ground black pepper

» 1 garlic clove, quartered

» ⅓ cup/13 g packed fresh mint leaves, from about 6 sprigs

» 2 tbsp coarsely chopped fresh flat-leaf parsley

» 2 tbsp extra-virgin olive oil

» ½ cup/55 g dried bread crumbs

» 2 tbsp Dijon mustard

Season the meaty parts of the lamb racks with the salt and pepper. Put each of the seasoned racks into its own cooking pouch. Seal the bags to 90 percent vacuum (dry setting on a FoodSaver machine). Refrigerate until you are ready to sous vide the meat.

Set the sous vide cooker to 130°F/54.4°C. If you are using a cooker with a circulator, close the rear pump flow switch and set the front switch to fully open. When the water bath reaches temperature, add the vacuum bags and cook for at least 1 hour, but the racks will not overcook if left in the water for up to 4 hours.

While the racks are slow-cooking, combine the garlic, mint, and parsley in the work bowl of a food processor and chop finely. Add the oil and the bread crumbs and process until the mixture is uniform, pale green, and moist enough to stick together but not wet. Remove to a sheet pan and set aside.

Preheat oven to 475°F/240°C/gas 9.

When the racks are done slow-cooking, remove the pouches from the water bath, snip open the sealed ends, and slip the racks from the bags. Pat the racks dry and brush all over with mustard. Roll the mustard-coated racks in the crumb mixture. Wipe off any excess crumbs from the sheet pan. Put the racks bone-side down on the pan and roast in the preheated oven until the crumbs are flecked with brown, about 8 minutes.

Carve into 8 double chops (see box, facing page) and serve.

CARVING A RACK OF LAMB AND CARVING A BONE-IN LEG

To Carve a Rack of Lamb:

Place the rack bones-side up on a cutting board. With a sharp carving knife, cut between every other bone, so you end up with two bones per chop.

To Carve a Bone-in Leg:

Put the lamb on its side and, starting on the outside, cut slices parallel to the bone until you reach the bone.

Turn the leg onto its cut side. Starting at the thicker end, cut slices perpendicular to the bone. You won't hit bone for the first few slices. Once you hit bone, continue to slice through the meat above the bone until you get to the end of the leg.

Separate the slices from the bone by making a long horizontal slice down the length of the bone.

SOUS VIDE
"BACON" AND EGGS

This reimagining of the classic American breakfast takes a long time but little work, and is suitable for the most elaborate brunch, or a casual sophisticated supper. The bacon is uncured pork belly, seasoned overnight with a smoky rub, and the eggs are soft-cooked in sous vide just until the yolk flows like heavy cream. By setting the sous vide precisely at 145.5°F/63°C, you get a soft, barely firm egg white enrobing its globe of yolk on the verge of release. The two are served with toast and a mound of greens dressed with a simple vinaigrette.

CHILLING TIME: 12 hours **PREP TIME:** about 20 minutes	**COOKING TIME:** 8 to 12 hours to sous vide pork; 1 to 1½ hours to sous vide eggs	**STORE:** Store sealed seasoned pork (raw or cooked) for up to 2 days; eggs do not store well after cooking.	*Makes* **6** *servings*

SPECIAL EQUIPMENT

» **Vacuum sealer and 1 food-grade plastic cooking pouch, large enough to hold the pork belly in a single layer**

» **1 tbsp fine sea salt**
» **2 tbsp smoked paprika**
» **1 tbsp light brown sugar**
» **½ tsp garlic powder**
» **½ tsp chipotle chili powder**
» **½ tsp ground black pepper, preferably smoked**
» **1½ lb/680 g boneless skinless pork belly, cut in 4 rectangles, about 1½ in/4 cm wide by 4 in/ 10 cm long**
» **6 large or extra-large eggs**
» **1 tbsp extra-virgin olive oil**
» **2 tsp red wine vinegar**
» **2 cups/60 g spring mix salad greens**
» **2 tbsp mild vegetable oil, such as canola**
» **6 slices French bread, toasted**
» **Coarse sea salt and freshly ground black pepper**

Combine the salt, paprika, brown sugar, garlic powder, chili powder, and black pepper in a small bowl. Rub the spice mixture all over the pork belly. Place on a rack set on a sheet pan and refrigerate uncovered overnight, at least 12 hours.

Put the seasoned pork belly in a large cooking pouch. Seal the bag to 90 percent vacuum (dry setting on a FoodSaver machine). Refrigerate until you are ready to sous vide the meat.

Set the sous vide cooker to 180°F/82.2°C. If you are using a cooker with a circulator, close the rear pump flow switch and set the front switch to half open. When the water bath reaches temperature, add the vacuum bag and cook for at least 8 hours, but it will not overcook the pork to leave it in the water for up to 12 hours.

When the pork is done slow-cooking, remove the pouch from the water bath and cool. Turn the temperature of the sous vide down to 145.5°F/63°C. When the water bath is at the right temperature, lower the eggs (no need for vacuum sealing) into the bath with a slotted spoon and slow cook for 1 to 1½ hours.

Mix the olive oil and vinegar in a small bowl; set aside. Put the greens in a bowl large enough for tossing; refrigerate.

Meanwhile snip open the sealed end of the cooking pouch, slip the pork belly from the bag, and cut each length of pork belly into three serving-size pieces. Pat the pork dry and set aside.

When the eggs are done, heat the vegetable oil over high heat in a medium skillet. Brown the pork belly squares on all sides in the hot oil, about 40 seconds per side. Drain on paper towels.

Put a toast on each of six plates. Remove an egg from the water bath with a slotted spoon. Crack off the narrow end with a small spoon and slip the egg from its shell into a small bowl. Most of the white will be set and the yolk creamy. Lift the egg on a slotted spoon, leaving the loose egg white in the bowl; put the egg on the toast. Repeat with remaining eggs.

Whisk the dressing to combine and toss with the greens. Make a small mound of salad on each plate next to the egg. Put a portion of the pork on the plate overlapping the salad. Season everything with coarse sea salt and pepper and serve.

CHAPTER 9

· SLOW ·

SWEETS

As a restaurant chef, I was always looking for ways to streamline my day. One of my favorite tricks was to "work" at night by baking cheesecakes while I slept. I had figured out that since I baked cheesecakes and custards in a water bath, the maximum temperature in the pan couldn't get hotter than the boiling point of water (212°F/100°C), regardless of the temperature of the oven. So why not set the oven at 175°F/80°C and forget the water bath? When I tried it, the cheesecakes were pristine: creamy from end to end, no grainy edges, and no cracks. The only hitch: they took 8 hours to bake. Then the obvious struck me—that was just about the amount of time I was away from the kitchen at night, so I could get two or three menu items done while I slept. I've been slow-baking ever since.

The technique works for any sweets with a creamy rich consistency—cheesecakes, custards, puddings, and cream fillings, but it is also helpful for long-cooking, dense cakes such as fruit-and-nut cakes, which have a tendency to burn on the edges before they are baked through. Since then I have realized that there are other desserts that follow the same principles: old-fashioned steamed puddings, meringues, and candied fruit. Now I have an entire collection of sweets that ask nothing from me other than a good night's sleep.

RICE PUDDING

Most rice pudding is simmered, not baked. Stove top rice puddings are creamy and fluid; baked rice puddings are solid and substantial. But slow-baked rice puddings bridge the gap. Because the oven temperature is extremely low, the pudding custard sets delicately, staying relatively soft and creamy. Because the pudding remains liquid for a long time during the baking cycle, most of the rice sinks to the bottom, so you have to stir it up to combine the rice below with the creamy custard on top.

PREP TIME: 10 minutes	COOKING TIME: about 4 hours	STORE: for up to 4 days, covered in the refrigerator. Can be rewarmed briefly in a microwave.	Makes 6 TO 8 servings

» 1 tbsp unsalted butter
» ½ cup/100 g Arborio rice, rinsed
» ⅓ cup/55 g golden raisins
» 1 qt/960 ml whole milk
» ¾ cup/150 g sugar
» ½ tsp ground cinnamon
» 2 large eggs
» Pinch of salt
» 2 tsp vanilla extract

Preheat the oven to 200°F/95°C. Butter the interior of a 1½-qt/1.4-l pudding mold or soufflé dish. Add the rinsed rice and raisins, and set aside.

Heat the milk, half the sugar, and the cinnamon in a medium saucepan over medium heat, until bubbles form around the edge of the milk, about 5 minutes.

Meanwhile beat the eggs, remaining sugar, salt, and vanilla in a medium mixing bowl until well combined. Slowly pour one-third of the hot milk mixture into the eggs, stirring constantly. Continue to add the milk in thirds until everything is blended. Pour into the pudding mold and stir to distribute the rice and raisins.

Cover the top with heavy-duty foil and crimp the edges tightly. Bake until barely set, about 4 hours. Remove from the oven and cool until just warm. When cool, stir the pudding with a fork incorporating the creamy custard on the top with the more solid rice on the bottom. Serve immediately or store tightly covered in a refrigerator for up to 4 days. Serve at room temperature or chilled.

VARIATION: IN A SLOW COOKER
Follow the directions, putting the covered pudding mold in a 6-qt/5.7-l slow cooker. Pour enough boiling water into the crockery around the mold to reach 1 in/2.5 cm up the side. Cover the cooker, and cook for 4 hours on high until the custard is set.

STEAMED CORNMEAL
PUDDING
WITH OLIVES AND CANDIED ORANGE

This new-world take on an old-world dessert is completely my fault. I made it up, tested it to the nth degree, and stand behind its unashamed sweet and savory idiosyncrasies. It is constructed like a traditional steamed pudding, with salty olives and candied orange taking the dried fruit role, honey and rosemary stepping in for the toffee sauce, and silken grainy cornmeal playing the supporting starchy role typically taken by a flour-based pudding mixture. The totality is earthy and sophisticated.

CHILLING TIME: 45 minutes **PREP TIME:** 20 minutes	**COOKING TIME:** about 3 hours	**STORE:** for up to 2 days, covered in the refrigerator. Can be rewarmed briefly in a microwave.	*Makes* **6** *servings*

» 6 oz/170 g pitted Kalamata olives, finely chopped

» 6 oz/170 g candied orange peel, finely diced

» 1 cup/240 ml hot water

» 1 tsp baking soda

» 1 tbsp orange liqueur or vodka

FOR THE SAUCE:

» 2 cups/480 ml heavy (whipping) cream

» ¼ cup/50 g sugar

» ¼ cup/60 ml honey

» 2 tbsp finely chopped fresh rosemary

» ¼ tsp fine sea salt

» 1 tbsp unsalted butter

FOR THE PUDDING:

» 4 tbsp/55 g unsalted butter, at room temperature

» ¾ cup/150 g sugar

» 2 large eggs

» 1¼ cups/175 g yellow cornmeal

» 1 tsp baking powder

In a small saucepan over high heat, combine the olives, candied orange peel, and hot water and bring to a boil. Remove from the heat and stir in the baking soda and liqueur; set aside.

To make the sauce: Simmer the cream, sugar, honey, rosemary, and salt in a small saucepan until thick enough to coat a spoon, stirring constantly, about 5 minutes. Refrigerate for 30 minutes. Coat the pudding mold or soufflé dish with the 1 tbsp butter. Pour two-thirds of the sauce into the prepared mold and put in the freezer until the sauce is solid, about 15 minutes.

To assemble the pudding: Beat the room-temperature butter and sugar with an electric mixer or by hand with a wooden spoon in a large mixing bowl until creamy. Beat in the eggs until well combined. Sift the cornmeal and baking powder in a separate bowl, and mix into the creamed butter and egg mixture in two additions, alternating with the olive mixture in a single addition.

Spoon the pudding on top of the frozen sauce. Cover the top of the mold with heavy-duty aluminum foil and secure to the mold with some string or a rubber band.

Put the mold in a large saucepan and pour boiling water around the mold until the water comes about halfway up the side of the mold, making sure it does not touch the foil. Cover the pot and steam the pudding over low heat for 3 hours, adding more water if the level should drop by more than half. When done, the top of the pudding will be dry and the center will feel barely soft.

Remove the pudding mold from the water and cool for 5 minutes. Take off the foil. Run a knife around the edge of the pudding and invert onto a plate. Scrape any sauce clinging to the mold over the top of the pudding. Serve in wedges with the remaining sauce.

VARIATION: IN A SLOW COOKER

Prepare the pudding as described. Put the covered pudding mold in a 6-qt/5.7-l slow cooker. Add boiling water to the cooker halfway up the side of the mold. Cover the cooker and cook on high for 3 hours. Finish and serve as described.

STICKY
TOFFEE PUDDING

The most classic of British steamed puddings, sticky toffee can mean several things. Sticky toffee is another name for caramel sauce, which can be poured over plain sponge cake, or, as in this recipe, baked in a mold with dates, vanilla, and pudding amalgam. It is best eaten fresh and warm, although leftovers can be rejuvenated in a microwave or a warm oven.

CHILLING TIME: 45 minutes **PREP TIME:** 20 minutes	**COOKING TIME:** about 3 hours	**STORE:** for up to 2 days, covered in the refrigerator. Can be rewarmed briefly in a microwave.	*Makes* **6** *servings*

» **6 oz/170 g pitted dates, finely chopped**

» **1 cup/240 ml hot water**

» **1 tsp baking soda**

» **1 tsp vanilla extract**

FOR THE SAUCE:

» **2 cups/480 ml heavy (whipping) cream**

» **½ cup/100 g firmly packed light brown sugar**

» **1 tbsp molasses**

» **¼ tsp fine sea salt**

» **1 tbsp unsalted butter**

FOR THE PUDDING:

» **4 tbsp/55 g unsalted butter, at room temperature**

» **¾ cup/150 g granulated sugar**

» **2 large eggs**

» **1¼ cups/145 g all-purpose flour**

» **1 tsp baking powder**

In a small saucepan over high heat, combine the dates and hot water and bring to a boil. Remove from the heat and stir in the baking soda and vanilla; set aside.

To make the sauce: Simmer the cream, brown sugar, molasses, and salt in a small saucepan until thick enough to coat a spoon, stirring constantly, about 5 minutes. Refrigerate for 30 minutes. Coat the pudding mold or soufflé dish with the 1 tbsp butter. Pour two-thirds of the sauce into the prepared mold and put in the freezer, until the sauce is solid, about 15 minutes.

To assemble the pudding: Beat the room-temperature butter and sugar with an electric mixer or by hand with a wooden spoon in a large mixing bowl until creamy. Beat in the eggs until well combined. Sift the flour and baking powder in a separate bowl, and mix into the creamed butter and egg mixture in two additions, alternating with the date mixture in a single addition.

Spoon the pudding on top of the frozen sauce. Cover the top of the mold with heavy-duty aluminum foil and secure to the mold with some string or a rubber band.

Put the mold in a large saucepan and pour boiling water around the mold until the water comes about halfway up the side of the mold and does not touch the foil. Cover the pot and steam the pudding over low heat for 3 hours, adding more water if the level should drop by more than half. When done, the top of the pudding will be dry and the center will feel barely soft.

Remove the pudding mold from the water and cool for 5 minutes. Take off the foil. Run a knife around the edge of the pudding and invert onto a plate. Scrape any sauce clinging to the mold over the top of the pudding. Serve in wedges with the remaining sauce.

VARIATION: IN A SLOW COOKER

Prepare the pudding as described. Put the covered pudding mold in a 6-qt/5.7-l slow cooker. Add boiling water to the cooker halfway up the side of the mold. Cover the cooker and cook on high for 3 hours. Finish and serve as described.

STEAMED CHOCOLATE
PLUM PUDDING

This is not your great-great-grandmother's plum pudding. Although it employs a cooking method that hasn't changed since the advent of indoor plumbing, it is way less dense and far more flavorful than the Dickensian puddings of yore. Although I suggest serving it with whipped cream, it really isn't necessary. This pudding makes its own sauce that simmers on the bottom of the pudding mold while the pudding sets above it. When inverted, the molten sauce flows over the sides, cloaking the pudding from top to bottom.

PREP TIME: 20 minutes	**COOKING TIME: about 3 hours**	**STORE: for up to 2 days, covered in the refrigerator. Can be rewarmed briefly in a microwave.**	*Makes* **6** *servings*

» **12 pitted prunes, finely chopped**
» **½ cup/120 ml hot water**
» **½ tsp baking powder**
» **½ tsp baking soda**
» **1 tsp vanilla extract**

FOR THE SAUCE:

» **2 tbsp unsalted butter**
» **½ cup/100 g firmly packed light brown sugar**
» **½ cup/85 g semisweet chocolate (chopped bar chocolate or chips)**
» **⅓ cup/75 ml half-and-half or heavy (whipping) cream**

FOR THE PUDDING:

» **9 tbsp/130 g unsalted butter, at room temperature**
» **⅔ cup/130 g granulated sugar**
» **2 large eggs**
» **¾ cup/90 g all-purpose flour**
» **⅓ cup/35 g unsweetened cocoa powder**
» **½ cup/90 g chocolate chips**

» **Sweetened whipped cream for serving (optional)**

Mix the prunes, hot water, baking powder, baking soda, and vanilla in a small bowl; set aside for about 10 minutes.

To make the sauce: Heat the butter, brown sugar, chocolate, and half-and-half in a small saucepan until smooth, stirring constantly; set aside.

To assemble the pudding: Grease the pudding mold or soufflé dish with 1 tbsp of the butter; set aside. In a large bowl, beat the remaining butter and the sugar using an electric mixer set on medium-high, or by hand with a wooden spoon, until creamy. Beat in the eggs until well combined.

Sift together the flour and cocoa in a separate bowl, and mix into the creamed butter and egg mixture in two additions, alternating with the prune mixture in a single addition. Stir in the chocolate chips.

Pour the sauce into the prepared pudding mold. Spoon the pudding on top of the sauce. Cover the top of the mold with heavy-duty aluminum foil and secure to the mold with some string or a rubber band.

Put the mold in a large saucepan and pour boiling water around the mold until the water comes about halfway up the side of the mold and does not touch the foil. Cover the pot and steam the pudding over low heat for 3 hours, adding more water if the level should drop by more than half. When done, the top of the pudding will be dry and the center will feel barely soft.

Remove the pudding mold from the water and let cool for 5 minutes. Take off the foil. Run a knife around the edge of the pudding and invert onto a plate. Scrape any sauce clinging to the mold over the top of the pudding. Cut into wedges and serve with whipped cream, if desired.

VARIATION: IN A SLOW COOKER

Prepare the pudding as described. Put the covered pudding mold in a 6-qt/5.7-l slow cooker. Add boiling water to the cooker halfway up the side of the mold. Cover the cooker and cook on high for 3 hours. Finish and serve as described.

VARIATION: CHOCOLATE-DATE-NUT PUDDING

Substitute 12 finely chopped pitted dates for the prunes and 1 cup/115 g toasted walnuts for the chocolate chips.

TRIPLE-
CHOCOLATE
BYPASS

If the notion of "too much chocolate" is meaningless to you, the next recipe should stand as a reality check. The cake mixes up in seconds and bakes unattended for 4 hours. Don't worry about overbaking it. When you take it out of the oven, it will look like chocolate pudding. Let it cool, and then refrigerate it for several hours until it is firm. Serve in thin slices, preferably with some berries or slices of citrus to refresh your palate between bites.

PREP TIME: 15 minutes	**COOKING TIME:** about 4 hours	**STORE:** for up to 5 days, covered in the refrigerator	*Makes* **12** *servings*

» Vegetable oil spray

» 2 cups/480 ml heavy (whipping) cream or light cream

» 1 cup/200 g firmly packed light brown sugar

» 1 lb/455 g semisweet chocolate, coarsely chopped

» ¼ tsp fine sea salt

» 1 tbsp vanilla extract

» 1 tsp almond extract

» 8 large egg yolks

» Sweetened whipped cream for serving (optional)

» Raspberries, orange slices, or other fresh fruit for serving (optional)

Preheat the oven to 175°F/80°C. Coat the bottom and sides of an 8-in/20-cm round springform cake pan with vegetable oil spray and line the bottom with parchment paper or aluminum foil. Set aside.

In a large heavy saucepan, heat the cream and brown sugar until simmering. Turn the heat to low, add the chocolate, and stir until the chocolate is melted. Remove from heat and stir in the salt and the vanilla and almond extract until smooth. Mix in the egg yolks. Pour into the prepared pan.

Bake until the surface of the cake is solid but still feels soft in the center, about 4 hours. Take it out of the oven and cool to room temperature on a rack. Refrigerate until completely firm. Cut around the sides of the cake and remove the sides of the pan from the bottom. Invert the cake onto a plate, and remove the bottom of the pan and the paper or foil liner. Invert back onto a serving plate. Serve in thin slices with whipped cream and fruit, if desired.

FIG AND WALNUT

FRUIT CAKE

I hesitate calling this confection "fruit cake," because I know what that means to most of you—cloying, dank, and leaden, a perfumed doorstop—and this masterpiece is none of those things. It is substantial, packed with pounds of figs and walnuts, and has only enough batter to keep the fruit and nuts from falling apart. The result is closer to a cake-size energy bar—chewy, and crunchy, and wholesomely rich.

PREP TIME: 20 minutes	COOKING TIME: about 8 hours	STORE: for up to 1 week, in an airtight container at room temperature	Makes **12** servings

» Vegetable oil spray

» 1 lb/455 g walnut halves and pieces

» 1 lb/455 g dried figs, stems removed, quartered

» ¾ cup/90 g all-purpose flour

» ½ tsp baking powder

» ½ tsp fine sea salt

» 1 cup/200 g sugar

» 3 large eggs, lightly beaten

» 1 tsp vanilla extract

» ½ cup/75 g diced candied orange peel

» ¼ cup/60 ml walnut brandy, such as Nocello

Preheat the oven to 225°F/110°C/gas ¼. Coat the inside of a 9-by-13-in/23-by-33-cm baking pan with the vegetable oil spray; set aside. Toss walnuts and figs in a large mixing bowl; set aside.

Mix flour, baking powder, salt, and sugar in a medium bowl. Toss 3 tbsp of the dry ingredients with the nuts and fruit to coat.

Add the eggs and vanilla with the remaining dry ingredients and mix with a wooden spoon to form a smooth batter. Mix in the candied orange peel. Scrape into the nuts and fruit and toss with a rubber spatula until everything is evenly coated.

Scrape the batter-coated nuts and fruit into the prepared pan, wet your hands with cold water, and pack the nuts and fruit firmly into the pan. Set in the oven and bake for 8 hours until the top is golden brown and a skewer inserted into the center comes out clean. (An instant-read thermometer inserted in the center of the cake should register 215 to 225°F/101 to 110°C).

Remove the pan from the oven and spoon the brandy over top. Cool on a rack for 30 minutes. Run a knife around the edge to loosen, invert onto a rack, remove the pan, turn right-side up, and cool to room temperature.

VARIATION: IN A SLOW COOKER

You can "bake" this cake in a slow cooker; you will need a 1½-qt/1.5-l soufflé dish and a 6 qt/5.7 l or larger slow cooker. Once the batter is in the soufflé dish, put it in the slow cooker and cook on low for 6 hours.

LEMON CHEESECAKE

Cheesecake is baked custard in which cream cheese takes the place of milk. Like all custards, it sets at 180°F/82°C, and every degree it reaches above that point creates graininess, drying, and cracking.

The conventional wisdom for keeping cheesecakes and custards from overcooking is to bake them in a water bath. Because the water in the bath can only reach 212°F/100°C regardless of how hot the oven gets, it ensures that the temperature at the edge of the cake will never get too hot. But the principles of slow cooking offer a better idea. By lowering the oven temperature to 175°F/80°C, the protection of a water bath becomes redundant. And because the oven temperature is the same as the finished temperature of the cake, overcooking is impossible. The cake doesn't rise because the temperature is too low to make the air in the batter expand—which means you get a texture that is as creamy at its edge as it is at its heart. And because the cake bakes so slowly, it never cracks, it never dries out, and it never overbakes.

PREP TIME: 10 minutes	**COOKING TIME:** 8 to 10 hours	**STORE:** for up to 1 week, covered in the refrigerator	*Makes* **12** TO **16** *servings*

» Vegetable oil spray

» ½ cup/55 g cookie crumbs (see Note)

» 2 lb/910 g cream cheese, at room temperature

» 1 cup/200 g sugar

» 1 tbsp vanilla extract

» 1 tbsp lemon extract

» ¼ cup/60 ml Limoncello (page 208)

» 5 large eggs

Right before you're ready to go to bed, preheat the oven to 175°F/80°C. Coat the inside of a 9-in/23-cm cheesecake pan generously with vegetable oil spray. Add the cookie crumbs, and tip and turn the pan to coat the bottom and sides with the crumbs. Tap to remove any excess crumbs. Set aside.

In a large bowl with a wooden spoon, mix the cream cheese and sugar until smooth and soft, scraping the sides of the bowl and spoon, as necessary. Mix in the vanilla, lemon extract, Limoncello, and eggs until the batter is well blended. Pour the batter into the prepared pan and place in the oven. Clean up and go to bed.

When you awake, 8 to 10 hours later (the exact time doesn't matter), the cake will appear set, the top will have barely colored, and the surface will be flawless. Remove to a rack and cool in the pan for an hour, until the pan is cool enough to handle.

Cover with a sheet of plastic wrap or wax paper and an inverted plate; invert. Remove the pan and refrigerate upside down for at least 1 hour. If you need to leave the house, the cake can stay refrigerated in this way all day.

Invert a serving plate over the cheesecake and invert the whole thing. Remove the top plate and the paper. Cover and refrigerate. Cut with a long sharp knife dipped in warm water to prevent sticking.

NOTE: *To make cookie crumbs, break up 5 or 6 plain shortbread or vanilla wafer cookies in a zippered plastic bag. Seal the bag and crush the cookies into crumbs using a rolling pin. Or if you want to automate the process, break the cookies into a food processor and pulse until uniform fine crumbs form. Be careful not to overprocess or the crumbs will get gummy.*

VARIATION: CHOCOLATE CHIP CHEESECAKE
Follow the recipe, substituting chocolate cookie crumbs for vanilla cookie crumbs and brandy for the limoncello. Eliminate the lemon extract and sift ¼ cup/60 ml cocoa in with the sugar. Fold 2 cups/400 g mini chocolate chips into the batter at the end.

VARIATION: RICOTTA CHEESECAKE
Follow the recipe, substituting whole-milk ricotta cheese for 1½ lb/680 g of the cream cheese.

Limoncello

Limoncello is a lemon-flavored liqueur originating from the Amalfi Coast of Italy that is quite stylish, sublimely delicious—and pretty pricey. Happily, it's easy to make at home. Your only investment is a bunch of lemons (and all you need is the zest; the juice can be used for other recipes), a bottle of vodka, and (of course) some time—about 2 weeks. Store for up to 8 months, in an airtight container in a cool, dark place, such as a refrigerator or cellar.

Makes about 5 cups/1.2 l; serves 20

» **1 cup/100 g freshly grated lemon zest (from about 8 lemons)**
» **3 cups/720 ml vodka**
» **1 cup/200 g sugar**

Combine the lemon zest and 1½ cups/360 ml of the vodka in a 2-qt/2-l glass bottle or jar with a tight-fitting lid. Seal and store in a cool, dark place until well flavored, for 1 week, shaking the jar every few days.

When the lemon vodka is ready, combine the sugar and 2 cups/480 ml water in a small saucepan and bring to a boil over medium-high heat. Cook for 3 minutes, stirring to dissolve the sugar, then remove from the heat and let cool to room temperature. Add to the bottle along with the remaining 1½ cups/360 ml vodka. Seal and store in the same way for another week.

Strain out the lemon zest before using.

SLOW-AND-CREAMY BLACK-BOTTOM
BANANA CUSTARD PIE

Custard pies have an anatomy problem. The high heat needed to get the crust crispy ruins the custard filling. Usually this means making the custard separately on a stove top and adding it to the prebaked crust. I've streamlined the process: the crust starts baking at high heat, then the oven is turned down low, the pie shell is filled, and it bakes until the custard sets. I have included ingredients and directions for a meringue topping that glorifies this pie spectacularly. If you don't want to make it, you can serve the pie simply topped with a mound of sweetened whipped cream.

PREP TIME: 45 minutes	COOKING TIME: 3 to 6 hours	STORE: for up to 2 days, covered in the refrigerator	*Makes* **8** TO **10** *servings*

» 1 Flaky Pie Crust (page 211) or your favorite homemade or purchased crust
» ½ cup/85 g semisweet chocolate chips
» 4 ripe bananas
» 3 large egg yolks
» 1 cup/240 ml half-and-half
» 1 cup/200 g granulated sugar
» 2 tsp vanilla extract
» ¼ tsp freshly grated nutmeg
» ¼ tsp fine sea salt
» Sweetened whipped cream for serving (optional)

FOR THE MERINGUE TOPPING (OPTIONAL):
» 3 large egg whites
» ½ cup/95 g superfine sugar
» 1 tsp vanilla extract
» ¼ tsp cream of tartar

Preheat the oven to 400°F/200°C/gas 6. Roll out the pie crust on a floured work surface and line a 9- or 9½-in/23- or 24-cm deep-dish pie pan with the crust. Trim and crimp the edges and chill until hard in a freezer, about 5 minutes. Line the chilled pie shell with foil and pie weights (I use dried beans) and bake until the edges are set, about 10 minutes. Carefully lift the foil and weights and bake the shell until light brown and fully set, about 15 minutes more.

Remove from the oven and reduce the oven temperature to 175°F/80°C. Sprinkle the chocolate chips over the bottom of the shell. When they are melted, about 5 minutes, spread over the bottom of the pastry with a small spatula. Cool.

Meanwhile, peel and slice the bananas and put in the work bowl of a food processor with the egg yolks, half-and-half, granulated sugar, vanilla, nutmeg, and salt. Purée until completely smooth. Pour into the chocolate-lined pie shell and bake until the custard is set, between 3 and 6 hours (because the oven temperature is so low it will not overbake). Remove from the oven and cool completely, or refrigerate overnight, if desired. Serve topped with sweetened whipped cream or baked meringue (read on).

CONTINUED

If you are making the meringue topping: At least an hour before serving, set oven to 375°F/190°C/gas 5. On the stove top, set a pot (large enough to support a medium-size bowl from your mixer) filled with ½ in/12 mm water over medium heat. Beat the egg whites with a balloon whisk until foamy in the mixer bowl. Add the superfine sugar a few spoonfuls at a time, continuing to beat lightly. Put the bowl over the hot water on the stove, and continue to mix until the egg whites become hot enough (about 115°F/46°C) to dissolve the sugar. The mixing does not need to vigorous but it should be active. The aim is not to incorporate air, but to keep the egg whites from cooking.

When the sugar is dissolved, in about 3 minutes, add the vanilla and cream of tartar. Beat with the electric mixer, fitted with a whisk attachment, gradually increasing the speed until a thick glossy meringue forms, about 3 minutes. Spoon the meringue onto the cooled pie filling, spreading it gently with the back of a spoon until the entire surface is covered and the edges of the meringue are anchored to the lip of the crust all of the way around, no gaps allowed. Make peaks in the meringue using the back of the spoon. Put the pie in the oven and bake until the peaks of the meringue are browned, about 6 minutes. Cool for 1 hour before serving. Serve in slices.

Flaky Pie Crust

The flakiness of a pie crust is determined not so much by the amount of shortening or type of fat (butter or lard) in the recipe, but how finely the shortening is dispersed in the flour before water is added. If it is cut in completely so that all of the flour is moistened with fat, the flake will be very small and the pastry is said to be "short," as is the case of shortbread. Keep the butter in bigger pieces and the flour forms bigger flakes when the water is added to the recipe. Such a pastry is "long flake."

Makes one 9- or 9½-in/23- or 24-cm deep-dish pie crust

» **1½ cups/175 g all-purpose flour**
» **¼ tsp fine sea salt**
» **1 tbsp sugar**
» **½ cup/115 g cold unsalted butter, cut into small pieces**
» **¼ cup/60 ml ice water**

Mix the flour, salt, and sugar in a mixing bowl. Add the butter and quickly toss to coat with flour. Working with your fingertips, pinch the butter pieces to break them up into tiny bits the size of puffed rice kernels. Try to work quickly and to touch the butter gingerly so the warmth of your skin doesn't melt it.

Drizzle the dry ingredients with ice water and continue pinching until all of the dry ingredients are moistened but are still in bits and pieces. Stop pinching! Quickly form the dough into a flat disk and wrap in plastic. Refrigerate for at least 1 hour. Use as directed in a recipe.

MERINGUE COOKIES

Meringues are always slow-baked. Because they are very sweet, high heat burns them, and moderate heat may brown them nicely but leaves them chewy and damp rather than crisp and airy, which is their intended destiny. Like all meringue cookies, these are gluten- and fat-free (except for the oil in the pine nuts), and if kept tightly sealed at room temperature, they will stay fresh for longer than you will be able to resist nibbling them.

PREP TIME: 20 minutes	COOKING TIME: about 2 hours	STORE: for up to 4 days, covered at room temperature	*Makes* **1 DOZEN** *cookies*

» 3 extra-large egg whites

» ¼ tsp cream of tartar

» ¼ tsp almond extract

» Pinch of fine sea salt

» ¾ cup/150 g superfine sugar (see Note)

» ½ cup/60 g pine nuts, chopped

Preheat the oven to 200°F/95°C and place a rack in the center of the oven. Line a baking sheet with parchment paper.

Beat the egg whites with an electric mixer until foamy. Add the cream of tartar and beat on medium-high until the whites form soft peaks. Add the almond extract, salt, and sugar, a few tablespoons at a time, and beat until the meringue is firm and glossy.

Spoon 2-in/5-cm mounds of meringue on the parchment in rows. It is helpful to have two spoons, one to lift the batter and one to scrape it onto the parchment. If you find that the parchment slides around as you are working, you can "glue" it to the baking sheet with a little meringue under each corner. Sprinkle the top of each cookie with chopped pine nuts.

Bake until pale colored and crisp, about 2 hours. Turn off the oven and leave the meringues to cool gradually in the oven for several hours or overnight. Store at room temperature.

NOTE: *If you don't have superfine sugar, you can make it by finely grinding ¾ cup + 1 tsp/150 g granulated sugar in a food processor.*

MARMALADE

Marmalade is the easiest of preserves, because citrus fruit is naturally high in pectin, the thickener of all jams, jellies, and preserves. The only work in this effortless recipe is slicing the oranges.

PREP TIME: 15 minutes	COOKING TIME: about 4 hours	STORE: for up to 2 months, in an airtight container in the refrigerator	*Makes* **1** *pint*

» 1 cup/200 g sugar

» 8 juice oranges, cut into ¼-in/6-mm slices

» 2 tbsp orange liqueur

Preheat the oven to 200°F/95°C.

Scatter ⅓ cup/65 g of the sugar over the bottom of a 2-qt/2-l glass baking dish. Layer the orange slices over the sugar and scatter the remaining sugar over top. Cover the dish tightly with foil and cook for 4 hours until the orange peels are tender and a syrup has formed in the baking dish.

Stir in the liqueur and cool to room temperature. Chop finely and store in a tightly closed container in the refrigerator.

VARIATION: IN A SLOW COOKER

Follow the recipe, layering the orange slices and sugar in a 3- to 4-qt/2.5- to 3.5-l slow cooker. Put a folded flat-weave kitchen towel over the top of the crock, cover, and cook on high for 4 hours.

ALMOND-STUFFED
~ APRICOTS ~
CANDIED IN AMARETTO SYRUP

Candying fruit takes patience and resolve, requiring repetitive rounds of simmering in sugar syrup until the fruit exchanges its natural juices for others that have been inundated with sugar. But by starting with dried fruit that is naturally thirsty for hydration, the process becomes streamlined. You just make a syrup, add the fruit, and let nature take its course. Serve warm or as a garnish with ice cream, pound cake, pudding, cheesecake, you name it.

CHILLING TIME: 1 hour **PREP TIME:** 45 minutes	**COOKING TIME:** about 2 hours	**STORE:** for up to 2 months, in an airtight container in the refrigerator	*Makes about 80 apricots; serves about 15*

- » 2 cups/340 g almonds
- » ¼ cup/50 g firmly packed light brown sugar
- » 1 large egg white
- » ¼ tsp almond extract
- » 2 lb/910 g dried whole large apricots

FOR THE SYRUP:
- » 3 cups/600 g granulated sugar
- » 3 cups/720 ml amaretto
- » 1 tbsp sherry vinegar
- » Pinch of fine sea salt

Put the almonds in a food processor and pulse carefully to a coarse meal. (Do not overprocess or you will have nut butter.) Add the brown sugar and continue to process until the mixture is uniformly fine. Add the egg white and the almond extract and process until the mixture forms a ball. Scrape from the processor and form into a ½-in/12-mm log. Wrap in plastic and refrigerate until firm, about 1 hour.

Slit open the apricots to form a pocket in the center of each; set aside.

Cut the almond paste into thin slices and roll each slice into a small ball. Insert a ball into the center of each apricot and push the cut edge of the apricot around the stuffing.

To make the syrup: Combine the granulated sugar, amaretto, vinegar, and salt in a medium saucepan and bring to a boil.

Carefully put the stuffed apricots in the hot syrup. Stir gently to submerge all of the fruit. Reduce heat to a simmer, cover the pan, and poach until the apricots are swollen, silky soft, and the stuffing is set, about 2 hours. Let cool in the syrup and store in the refrigerator.

INDEX